OXFORD MEDICAL PUBLICATIONS

Quality Improvement by Peer Review

OXFORD GENERAL PRACTICE SERIES

6.   The consultation: an approach to learning and teaching
     David Pendleton, Theo Schofield, Peter Tate and Peter Havelock
9.   Modern obstetrics in general practice
     Edited by G. N. Marsh
11. Rheumatology for general practitioners
     H. L. F. Currey and Sally Hull
13. Paediatric problems in general practice (second edition)
     Michael Modell and Robert Boyd
15. Psychological problems in general practice
     A. C. Markus, C. Murray Parkes, P. Tomson, and M. Johnston
17. Family problems
     Peter R. Williams
18. Health care for Asians
     Edited by Bryan R. McAvoy and Liam J. Donaldson
19. Continuing care: the management of chronic disease (second edition)
     Edited by John Hasler and Theo Schofield
20. Geriatric problems in general practice (second edition)
     G. K. Wilcock, J. A. M. Gray, and M. J. Longmore
21. Efficient care in general practice
     G. N. Marsh
22. Hospital referrals
     Edited by Martin Roland and Angela Coulter
23. Prevention in general practice (second edition)
     Edited by Godfrey Fowler, Muir Gray, and Peter Anderson
24. Women's problems in general practice (third edition)
     Edited by Ann McPherson
25. Medical audit in primary health care
     Edited by Martin Lawrence and Theo Schofield
26. Gastrointestinal problems in general practice
     Edited by Roger Jones
27. Domiciliary palliative care
     Derek Doyle
28. Critical reading for primary care
     Edited by Roger Jones and Ann-Louise Kinmonth
29. Research methods and audit in general practice
     David Armstrong and John Grace
30. Counselling in primary health care
     Edited by Jane Keithley and Geoffrey Marsh
31. Professional education for general practice
     Peter Havelock, John Hasler, Richard Flew, Donald McIntyre, Theo Schofield, and John Toby
32. Quality improvement by peer review
     Richard Grol and Martin Lawrence

Quality Improvement by Peer Review

Oxford General Practice Series • 32

RICHARD GROL
Universities of Nijmegen and Maastricht, The Netherlands

and

MARTIN LAWRENCE
University Department of Public Health and Primary Care, Oxford

With assistance and contributions from:

W. van Beurden   H. Mokkink
J. Dalhuysen   I. Smeele
J. Derry   T. Toemen
P. van de Hombergh   V. Tielens
A. Zwaard

OXFORD   NEW YORK   TOKYO
OXFORD UNIVERSITY PRESS
1995

Oxford University Press, Walton Street, Oxford OX2 6DP
Oxford   New York   Toronto
Delhi   Bombay   Calcutta   Madras   Karachi
Kuala Lumpur   Singapore   Hong Kong   Tokyo
Nairobi   Dar es Salaam   Cape Town
Melbourne   Auckland   Madrid

and associated companies in
Berlin   Ibadan

Oxford is a trade mark of Oxford University Press

Published in the United States
by Oxford University Press Inc., New York

A catalogue record for this book is available from the British Library

Library of Congress Cataloging in Publication Data
(Data available upon request)

ISBN 0 19 262521 7

Typeset by EXPO Holdings, Malaysia

Printed in Great Britain by Redwood Books, Trowbridge, Wilts.

The reluctance of people to have their work evaluated is closely linked with their reluctance to comment on, or to complain about the behaviour of others. Most people 'live and let live'. This attitude, we admit, is not only understandable: it is invaluable. Social life depends on it. Who should throw the first stone? Who indeed can really distinguish between an honest mistake and culpable negligence? This is why we believe that efforts to improve performance must come from a desire for self-improvement, a desire based on an essentially ethical insight. Audit must not be part of a disciplinary instrument; it must be a tool for learning by feedback.

N. McIntyre and K. Popper (1983)

Preface

Medical audit has recently become a way of life in the UK, with general practitioners (GPs) and practices obliged to perform regular data collection and audit activities. In other countries there is also increasing activity in the field of evaluation of general practice. Medical audit has become a popular method of quality assurance. Not everyone, however, is convinced of the effectiveness of this approach (Morrell 1991). The emphasis is all too often on comparing performance data with standards presented by policy-makers, and not on improvement of performance in practice, based on the motivation of care providers.

The increasing drive for improvement in the quality of care demands practical, GP-friendly, and acceptable methods. Research into their needs and preferences (Pickup 1983; Shirrifs 1989; Cervero 1981; Branthwaite 1988; Owen *et al.* 1989; Forrest *et al.* 1989) has shown that GPs prefer education that is:

- close to the practice;
- in small groups of respected colleagues;
- with personal contact and active participation;
- not too time consuming;
- reflecting on and reviewing personal performance;
- offering new information or skills;
- aiming to reduce the uncertainty and elevate the status of their work.

Peer audit or peer review with an educational goal may satisfy these needs (Grol 1990b). Research has shown that a combination of activities and interventions over an extended period is a particularly effective method of inducing change and improvement in practice, and that evaluation and support by peers should be the core of these activities (Lomas and Haynes 1988; Soumerai *et al.* 1990; Grol 1992). Peer review is appropriate both in countries such as the UK where most primary care is based in group practice, and education is increasingly based in that group setting; and in most other European countries where practitioners are often single handed and join groups outside their practice for educational activity. In this book methods for both types of peer review are presented.

The aim of this book is to broaden the perspective of audit as it is performed now in the UK and many other countries. The current emphasis on collecting data, preventive care, chart review, and analysis of practice activities may inhibit real improvement in patient care and may be counterproductive. Experiences with quality improvement by means of formal assessment in the USA have made many of the experts there very suspicious. Berwick (1989) wrote about this approach that 'relying on inspection to improve quality is at best inefficient and at worst a formula for failure'. His message is that an overall system for quality improvement is required in which audit has a limited, but necessary role (Berwick 1992, Berwick *et al.* 1992, Deming 1986). Quality improvement by peer review is a key element in such a system.

Moreover the awareness has grown that the motivation for improvement has first to be present or be developed in individual care providers. They need a feeling of professional responsibility to account for their work to themselves and others (Irvine 1990). Peer review, medical audit between peers in a safe setting, has been recommended as a means of achieving this in a recent statement on quality assurance by WONCA, the world organisation of Family Doctors (Marwick *et al.* 1992). This recommends that GPs and members of their practices come together, exchange their experiences, assess each other's daily work with patients using explicit and acceptable criteria, and help each other to achieve the necessary changes.

A previous version of this book (Grol 1988) received many positive reactions from doctors in many countries. Therefore the decision was made to write a new version, adapted to recent insights in and experiences with peer review and quality improvement and to the current demands on GPs in the UK and other countries.

The book contributes to the knowledge, attitudes, and skills which providers of primary care need to develop when undertaking quality assurance with their colleagues. The methods are based on audit and peer review projects undertaken in The Netherlands and the UK in the last decade. Hundreds of GPs participated in these projects and evaluated the methods. Generally they were very positive. Many GPs experienced participation as having given new joy to their daily practice work (Grol 1988*a*). The book does not pretend to cover the whole complex audit spectrum. It is focused primarily on helping GPs and primary care workers in learning together in small groups of peers, and on the dynamics of and procedures for this activity.

As part of the group work, panels of GPs and social scientists formulated practical instruments and guidelines for use in peer review. They were discussed in peer review groups, adapted, and used for setting individual or group targets. Examples of these instruments and guidelines are offered in this book. They are indeed guidelines, they are not absolute. They represent common ideas on adequate performance in general practice. They are meant as a help, as a tool for critical reflection, not more and not less than that. They can be adapted to local circumstances, and used to develop more specific protocols, to derive criteria on which to evaluate performance, and to set target standards.

WHO MAY BENEFIT FROM THIS BOOK?

The book offers both the theory and practice of peer review. It is intended particularly to be used by general practitioners as well as their fellow care providers in primary care teams. It will be appropriate in vocational training, when trainers and trainees wish to introduce peer review into their educational activities. It will also be a useful guide for managers and policy-makers wishing to set up or support quality improvement in their local situations.

The process described is very relevant for use in countries such as the UK where much education and development take place within practice teams. Peer review is also increasingly seen as a key method for networking and improvement in other countries where general practitioners are often more isolated and seek continuing education outside the practice in a group setting.

CONTENT OF THE BOOK

The book is organized in the following manner. It has three parts: one on the theoretical background of peer review, one on various methods for peer review, and one offering instruments and guidelines for the application of peer review activities.

I.   In this part the *nature of peer review* is described. In the first chapter a definition of peer review is given as well as a stepwise model for applying it. Chapter 2 gives more detail on the use of guidelines in peer review. Chapter 3 offers an overview of methods that may be used in assessing practices' and practitioners' performance. Chapter 4 is on change and improvement through peer review. This part of the book ends with an overview of research into the effectiveness of peer review (Chapter 5) and a description of the conditions necessary for the smooth running of a peer review process (Chapter 6).

II. In the second part of the book *various methods for peer review* are presented. Chapter 7 offers some general principles. The following chapters describe the setting of guidelines in peer review (8); the use of audio- or videotaped consultations in small groups (9); the use of data on clinical performance in peer review (10); and the methods of case analysis, mutual practice observation, and practice-based quality circles (11–12). This part of the book ends with instructions for supervisors of peer review groups (13).

III. The last part is devoted to *instruments and guidelines* for practice that can be used in peer review activities. These cover general consultation skills (14), clinical performance in common conditions (15), patient education (16), and practice management (17).

We would like to thank Agnes de Grunt, Myriam Kassies, and Penny Callaghan for their important contribution in the development of the manuscript for this book.

Nijmegen	R.G.
Oxford	M.L
January 1995	

Contents

Part I

Peer review: an orientation

The most fruitful lesson is the
conquest of one's own error.
Whoever refuses to admit error
may be a great scholar, but he
is not a great learner.

Wolfgang Goethe

1 A model for peer review and audit

INTRODUCTION AND DEFINITIONS

Medical audit and peer review are concepts which have gradually gained currency among general practitioners, although many do not know exactly what is meant by these terms nor what they involve precisely. The many terms related to audit have reached a stage where they can be seen merely as confusing jargon (Shaw 1980): clinical audit, peer audit, quality assessment, quality control, quality improvement, quality assurance, quality management, etc.

We favour the terms quality assurance or quality improvement by which is meant (Black 1990): 'Quality assurance is concerned with the assessment of quality of medical care, the efforts to improve the provision of that care and the procedures to ensure that good quality is maintained.' This is similar to the WONCA definition of quality assurance as a 'process of planned activities based on performance review and enhancement with the aim of continually improving standards of patient care' (Marwick 1992).

A further difficulty is the different use of terminology on each side of the Atlantic. In Europe 'quality assurance' is the more commonly used term, often synonymously with 'quality improvement'. In the USA only 'quality improvement' is used for this type of activity, and 'quality assurance' is considered as a retrospective review activity rather in the way that we in Europe tend to use the word 'audit'.

Medical audit can be seen as a subset of quality improvement, wherein one topic is handled at a time. As Sheldon (1982) put it, 'Medical audit is the study of *some part* of the structure, process and outcome of medical care, carried out by those personally involved, to measure whether set objectives have been attained, and thus assess the quality of care given.'

A major restriction in the perception of audit has sometimes been the lack of emphasis on improvement within the concept—indeed Sheldon himself does not mention improvement. But most authors include improvement within their definitions (Irvine 1991). Thus quality improvement includes a wide variety of activities—setting priorities, choosing topics, training staff, assessing patients' needs—but audit is an essential component.

One further point. Usage commonly reserves 'medical audit' for audit involving only doctors, and 'clinical audit' for audit involving all healthcare workers. In the multidisciplinary context of modern primary care there is little relevance for a 'doctors only' exercise, and in this book medical audit and clinical audit in primary care are regarded as synonymous.

Peer review is offered in this book as a method for implementing quality improvement or medical audit. It is best described as 'Continuous, systematic and critical reflection on their own and others' performance by a number of colleagues in general practice, with the aim of achieving a continuous improvement in the quality of patient care.' Peer review is then an ongoing process involving the defining of criteria, evaluating performance, and implementing change; it focuses on continuous change and mainly uses prospective methods. For example, improvement in audit is to be expected from peer review as data are fed back on gaps in performance. But it must not be forgotten that audit is but one aspect of quality improvement.

Audit	*Quality improvement*
• project based	• continuous activities
• aims to control a specific problem	• continuous change
• mainly retrospective	• mainly prospective
• emphasis on data collection and feedback	• emphasis on colleagues' support

'look at where you are'   'look at where you want to be'

A 'peer' is a person who is equal in any stated respect (Irvine 1991). In the context of medical audit the word applies to a person working in the same branch of medicine, who has comparable experience and training. In this book we want to use the term 'peer' in a rather broad manner and include:

• principals and trainees in a health centre or a practice;
• GPs working together in local or regional groups;
• colleagues of different disciplines working together in a practice or a health centre.

Example: peer review of hypertension management

A primary healthcare team worked on the management of hypertension in the following manner (after Williamson 1992):

• Selecting the topic: at a meeting of all the members of staff, possible problems in care provision were discussed critically. The supervision of hypertensive patients was selected as a priority.
• Formulating criteria: the team selected the diastolic blood pressure (DBP) level as a relevant indicator for quality of care and defined as a criterion that a level of <95 mmHg would be acceptable; a target standard was set that 95 per cent of the hypertensive patients had to achieve this level.
• Evaluation of care: review of the records of 215 patients showed that 54 per cent of the patients had DBP in accordance with the criterion.
• Planning and implementing change: an analysis of possible barriers to achieving the criterion was made by some members of the team. The conclusion was that the GPs were inadequately aware of the non-compliance of their patients and that the patients had inadequate insight into their condition and treatment. During the group meetings GPs and

practice assistants trained each other in giving better education to hyper-tensive patients and in better supervision of these patients.

- Follow-up: 12 months after the training a new audit took place: 25 per cent of the patients did not meet the criterion. The results were discussed in the peer group and the team decided to start specific clinics for hyper-tensive patients, with much attention to patient education and guidance. A new follow-up evaluation showed a further reduction to 17 per cent in the number failing to meet the criterion. The group members decided that further improvement would be too expensive and moved on a new relevant problem.

LEARNING BY PEER REVIEW

Quality assurance can be performed externally (by policy-makers, insurers, patients, or external boards) or internally, by the profession itself. It can be aimed at selection and control (for example, relicensing, accreditation, or budgeting). It can also be educational, focused on the learning and improvement process of general practition-ers and their practices. Peer review is seen here primarily as a systematic quality improvement activity for general practitioners and other care providers in general practice, a method for learning and changing (Batstone 1990). It differs from classic continuing education in the use of explicit criteria for good quality of care, in the collection of data on individual and practice performance, and in the development and implementation of a plan for changes in practice. This type of education is an important learning tool for medical professionals. The opinions of many GPs and the results of many studies show that in particular assessment, feedback, and support by respected peers in a safe setting will offer a very powerful stimulus for change (see also Chapter 5). In many countries positive experiences have been gained with peer review in groups of GPs, in vocational training as well as with practising GPs. These experiences showed that:

- Setting up peer review in practices and in small groups of practitioners is possible.
- It can be a very motivating activity for health professionals in primary care; it can help practitioners break through the isolation in which they frequently have to operate; it improves the mutual involvement and commitment of care providers to each other's work.
- It has proven to be one of the favourite educational methods for busy practitioners.
- It can bring about real lasting changes in practice performance.

There is now an increasing awareness that classic continuing medical education cannot solve the existing problems in healthcare. The performance of care providers becomes routine very quickly after graduation and does not change if there is no room for regular critical reflection on this performance and no support from colleagues.

AIMS OF PEER REVIEW

Different providers in healthcare may have different aims with regard to quality improvement in general practice and therefore also with peer review activities. Uses of peer review may include:

- a method to support daily practice work;
- a tool in changing practice performance;
- a way to reduce inter-doctor or inter-practice variation;
- a tool in reaccredition of GPs;
- a tool in contracting arrangements;
- a prerequisite for becoming a trainer or a member of a college of GPs or practitioners;
- a stimulus for individual learning.

Care providers will tend to emphasize 'educational' goals for peer review, while policy-makers and funders generally will focus at discrete goals where attainment can be measured. The *aims* of peer review should therefore *be very clear* from the very beginning in order to prevent fear, misunderstanding, and resistance from the care providers involved. We believe that it should mainly *be used as an educational* tool in improving patient care. Berwick (1989) wrote that there is no external evaluation system that is sound enough to survive the fear of the people who are being evaluated. Peer review on a confidential and educational basis may reduce this fear as far as possible.

A MODEL FOR PEER REVIEW

In the literature widespread agreement is found on the steps which must be taken in medical audit (Lawrence and Schofield 1993; Irvine 1991):

- agree criteria, set target standards;
- observe practice, collect data on performance;
- evaluate information, assess performance against criteria or targets;
- plan care, identify needs for change, implement change.

These steps are part of a cycle of continuous quality improvement (Fig. 1.1). But eventually each step will need to be discussed and undertaken.

1.   Choosing a topic, stating priorities—'What do we want to review?'

The range of subjects in general practice suitable for audit is extremely wide reaching. One is forced to state priorities and choose subjects which are important for general practice care, which are definable, which occur frequently in daily care, and which are amenable to change. Subjects can be divided into (Donabedian 1980):

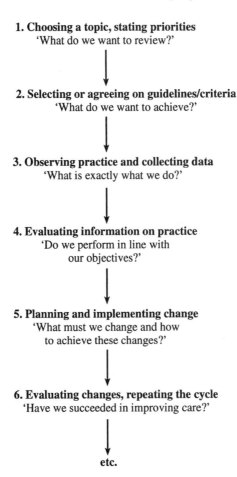

Fig. 1.1   A stepwise model for peer review.

- review of structural aspects of general practice care: organization of the practice, resources, recording systems, collaboration within the practice and with other care providers, management of the practice, etc.;
- review of the process of providing care: clinical performance (examination, referrals, prescriptions, medical decision-making), interpersonal performance (communication, education of patients), managerial performance (accessibility, continuity);
- review of the outcomes of care: the effects of care on the health, the well-being, the illness behaviour, and the satisfaction of patients; the costs of care are also frequently seen as an outcome.

In this book all aspects get some attention, although the emphasis is on process aspects.

2.   Selecting or agreeing on guidelines for care and criteria for evaluation— 'What do we want to achieve?'

Most writers on quality assurance agree that it is essential to formulate explicit guidelines for care and criteria for the assessment of the quality of care. Generally, these concern statements on desirable performance or outcomes, which have been discussed among GPs or practice workers and about which there is a certain degree of consensus at the time in question. (More information on the use of guidelines and criteria in peer review is presented in Chapter 2.) Guidelines for care may be based on various sources (for example, The British Thoracic Society guidelines for management of asthma). A peer group may also attempt to formulate their own guidelines, but one should remember that this is a time-consuming exercise that demands considerable skills (North of England Study 1992). Criteria for evaluation may be concerned with optimal, with average, or with minimal performance depending on the stringency of the performance and the level of attainment expected. Average performance is generally seen as acceptable for most GPs, but there is the danger of opting for the *status quo*. In this book some criteria suitable for assessing optimal performance are presented, as examples. They are not meant to be prescriptive, they are particularly meant for reflection and as a help in developing target standards for improvement by individual care providers and practices.

3.   Observing practice and collecting data—'What exactly are we doing?'

The next step in the cycle is recording in detail the care offered in the practice and the activities performed by the healthcare providers. There is a great number of methods available for this purpose: monitoring the performance with the aid of specially designed checklists; retrospective examination of medical records; observation of a colleague's practice; audio- or videotaping of consultations; using simulated patients; using aggregated data from registration systems or insurance companies, etc. More information on this topic is presented in Chapter 3.

4.   Evaluating information on practice—'Is our performance in line with our targets?'

The analysis of the information, comparing actual care with the defined targets, comparing care of one GP with other GPs and one practice with other practices, and providing feedback to each other on the results of these activities, actually form the essence, the heart of the review process. This enables the GP to identify shortcomings in approach and to become aware of inadequate practice performance. At the same time it shows which elements are being carried out adequately. In this way a personal process of awareness, learning, and change is set in motion. Understandable, well-organized feedback is crucial in this process.

5.   Planning and implementing change—'What must we change, and how can we achieve change?'

Discrepancy between actual performance and agreed targets for good practice care can be a stimulus for change. This implies in the first place the acceptance of the targets and the feedback as relevant and feasible for daily care. Changes should be seen as desirable or necessary. Specific feasible changes for practice should be selected. With support of the peer group, a plan for implementing these changes should be developed. Colleagues can support each other in this process by offering alternative practice styles, demonstrating new ways of working, and giving solutions to specific problems in the implementation of changes. More information on this topic is offered in Chapter 4.

6.   Evaluating changes, repeating the cycle—'Have we succeeded in improving care?'

Finally, information about performance is gathered once again to see if the GP or the practice has succeeded in bringing about the planned changes in the pattern of care offered to patients. It may be that the practice's guidelines are not feasible for day-to-day care; that they should be adapted and be made more realistic. It may also disclose that the GPs or the practice did not succeed in achieving their aims. An analysis of problems and barriers in implementing the desired changes has to be made. On the basis of this analysis a new plan for change can be developed with new interventions and activities. If selected objectives have been achieved, the peer group can choose a new topic for review. In this way, a group of colleagues works gradually, step by step, towards improvement of the quality of patient care.

MANAGING PEER REVIEW

To carry out the peer review process successfully, it is necessary to organize it carefully. This implies good preparation, teaching participants necessary skills, developing a positive attitude in the group, and taking good care of meeting arrangements (Chapter 6).

CONCLUSIONS

Peer review can be seen as a method for continuous quality assessment and improvement. In particular, the systematic reflection on each other's performance by colleagues, who respect each other and know the general practice situation well, may be a powerful stimulus for bringing about desirable change in patient care. A stepwise process has to be followed in peer review:

- choosing a topic;
- selecting or agreeing on criteria and target standards;
- observing practice, collecting data;
- evaluation of the information;
- planning and implementing change;
- evaluating changes.

Ideally, a practice or a local or regional group of health professionals goes through these steps continuously.

2 The use of guidelines and criteria in peer review

'Standards of care are not the same as standard care. Variety in the nature of care offered may well be desirable to allow choice, but there is no value in variety in quality. Nobody benefits from poor care.'

(Pendleton 1986)

INTRODUCTION

We have described peer review as a systematic assessment of one's own and one another's pattern of care with the aim of achieving a continuous improvement of patient care. In such a peer review process explicit guidelines for what is considered to be desirable general practice care play a central role. However, it is not unusual to find general practitioners objecting to clearly formulated guidelines and criteria and the uniformity they imply. This feeling of threat is increased by poor understanding of terminology which is often seen to imply external imposition when it does not.

DEFINITIONS OF GUIDELINES, PROTOCOLS, CRITERIA, AND STANDARDS

There are many definitions related to these terms. The area is about as confusing as the area of quality assurance and medical audit. But increasingly there is a strong tendency to use the term 'guidelines' to mean recommendations to help practitioners in their decisions on appropriate healthcare (Field 1990). This is useful, because such recommendations can be adapted by practitioners as appropriate to their local situation without being seen as being prescriptive. It enables practitioners to receive reasoned advice provided externally—and this is necessary in the efficient use of time and expertise. Practices may adapt guidelines into a form in which they agree to follow them—and such an agreed care plan can be termed a *protocol*.

But such guidelines and protocols are wide ranging and not suitable directly for evaluating actual practice performance. Precise and selective statements against which an assessment can be made are required in this situation. We will use the terms elements, indicators, criteria, and standards here (Lawrence and Schofield 1993; Donabedian 1986; see examples in Table 2.1).

- Any topic of care which we choose to assess consists of a large number of *elements*, so many that we must select a few for the purpose of assessment.

Table 2.1   *Examples of indicators, criteria, and standards for evaluating general practice care*

Example	Indicator	Criterion	Target standard
(a) Access	The length of time that a patient must wait for a non-urgent appointment with a particular doctor	That such a delay should not exceed 48 hours	That the criterion of less than 48 hour's delay should be achieved in 80% of requests
(b) Critical incident analysis	Sudden death under the age of 60	That a sudden death of a patient under age 60 should be discussed between peers in the practice at a meeting within a month of its occurrence	That the criterion is achieved in 90% of cases
(c) Diabetes			
Structure	That the diabetic patients in the practice should be identifiable	Each patient should be on a register of diabetics	100% of diabetes patients should be in the system
Process	Blood pressure should be monitored in diabetic patients	Blood pressure should be taken at least once a year	90% of patients should meet this criterion
Outcome	Value of blood glucose	Fasting blood sugar should be ≤8.00 mmol/l	80% of patients aged 25–74 should achieve this level

- The aim will be to base our assessment on those elements which are good *indicators* of the quality of care. A good indicator should be definable and measurable, be important in determining the outcome of care or a desired outcome itself, and be something that can be changed. Indicators thus identify the elements of care to be looked at.
- Such an element needs to be defined so precisely that it is possible to say whether it is present or absent. Elements defined so precisely can be referred to as *criteria*.
- Finally, having criteria formulated, it is possible to measure the extent to which a particular care provider or a practice succeeds in achieving these criteria.

When a GP or a practice sets a level of performance for the achievement of a criterion, we are talking about setting a *target standard* for quality of care.

We thus have guidelines (usually external) and protocols (usually practice agreed) as a basis for care; and criteria (often externally suggested) and target standards (usually practice agreed) on which to base evaluation.

One must be aware that criteria and standards can also be used for external assessment. We have described criteria as elements on which professionals can base target standards and guide performance and education. They can also be used to set external standards on the basis of which practice can be judged (for reimbursement) or controlled (for compliance with regulations).

THE NEED FOR GUIDELINES, PROTOCOLS, CRITERIA, AND STANDARDS

Owing to the fact that GPs have often worked in isolation for a long time and not received feedback on performance, they have generally developed their own implicit standards. They are satisfied with most of these and experience them as sufficiently effective in their care provision. General practitioners frequently regard explicit criteria coming from 'outside' as not relevant or realistic for their own situation.

Despite such reservations criteria and standards are quite indispensable in quality assurance and change in healthcare (Donabedian 1986; Irvine 1990; Leape 1990; Farmer 1991).

There are various reasons why the development of explicit practice protocols and targets is crucial for peer review (Table 2.2):

• Guidelines can be a support for health professionals in daily care. For the average GP it is almost impossible to keep up with all new developments and insights. Personal guidelines for care provision become outdated or obsolete very fast, without anyone realizing it or being aware of it. Interviews with GPs show that most of them have questions on the right approach in many common diagnostic and therapeutic decisions and have an open attitude to guidelines that provide good answers to such questions.

  Medical care is becoming increasingly complicated. Each practitioner is involved in about 20–30 daily contacts with different patients, each with different complaints and expectations. Practitioners have to decide, minute by minute, what the next step will be. They must take a whole series of major and minor decisions; hypotheses are constructed and weighed up; innumerable verbal and non-verbal messages are registered and evaluated. In order to cope with such complexity every GP recognizes the necessity of fixed patterns of reactions, which facilitate decision-making. Despite the fact that each contact with a patient is a new, unique event, the behaviour of healthcare providers brings to it a certain degree of consistency from encounter to encounter. These patterns of performance act as implicit guidelines for practitioners, based on experience and education. They represent the personal values of practitioners in their work. The essence of peer review is

Table 2.2   *Pros and cons of explicit practice guidelines and criteria*

Pro	Contra
Decrease undesirable variation in care by providers and practices	Force the care provider in a certain direction; decrease autonomy
Give a basis for the decisions of care providers	Situation of a patient is often unique and not suited for guidelines
Are a professional responsibility	
Are educational; give care providers clear objectives to work to	Local or regional differences make it difficult to formulate (consensus) guidelines
Help to clarify existing implicit criteria, used by care providers	Danger of abuse by patients, insurers, managers
Patients and society know better what to expect of general practice	Not much evidence that patient care is really improved by using guidelines
Help in demarcating the tasks of general practice and specialist care	Guidelines are generally too ideal and not suited for daily care
Are a guarantee to society that general practice takes quality seriously	There is generally no financial reward or support for following the guidelines; new guidelines ask for extra investment most of the time
Increase solidarity between GPs; enlarge the involvement with each other's work	
May improve cost-effective performance	
May protect care providers in malpractice suits	It is too difficult to change fixed routines in practice

reflecting on them, rendering them explicit, and comparing them with other guidelines, eventually enabling each practice or practitioner to develop an explicit protocol on the basis of which performance can be evaluated.

- Views and procedures differ considerably between physicians and practices; part of this variation can be attributed to differences in patient mix, another part might be an undesirable variation in provided care. If we see, for instance, that one GP has 10 times as many diabetes tests or 20 times as many repeat prescriptions as another we know that something might be wrong. By its very nature, wide variability indicates that some patients are receiving suboptimal care (Stolline and Weiner 1988). However, in order to interpret this variation correctly and to determine where improvement is needed, explicit criteria for good quality of care are necessary. They will help the peer review group in identifying the directions for change.

- Explicit guidelines may thus act as a point of reference for continuing education and for practice-based or local activities in bringing about change in general practice. At this moment the content of such activities generally depends on the ideas or interests of particular GPs or medical specialists or is a representation of vested interests of pharmaceutical companies. This is both confusing and undesirable for the profession. Explicit guidelines may yield a common policy for education and learning in general practice, because they highlight agreed areas of educational need at a particular time.

- Finally, explicit guidelines and practice protocols may be a good way to show and guarantee to 'outsiders' (patients, insurers, managers) that general practice takes quality seriously, that practitioners are able to account for their work. They may help to prevent expectations of patient care in general practice becoming unrealistic. They may also improve society's confidence in GPs and inhibit the tendency to interfere top-down.

METHODS FOR DEVELOPING GUIDELINES

Adequate and effective development of guidelines, criteria, and standards for practice demands some basic features (Grol 1993):

- A thorough procedure is needed for summarizing the available research evidence, for reaching consensus, and for drawing up the guidelines and criteria (Field 1990; Audet *et al.* 1990).
- Good practice guidelines are a mixture of scientific basis, clinical applicability, and feasibility in day-to-day care. For many aspects of general practice, scientific data are unavailable, controversial, or not immediately applicable in practice. So, clinical experience plays an important role. Testing of the guidelines in practice is also desirable.
- Guidelines and criteria should be developed at various levels, centrally as well as at local and practice level.

Roughly speaking there are two approaches to developing guidelines and criteria (Table 2.3), both of which have their advocates: the decentralized approach and the central approach.

A decentralized approach

A local group, a group practice, or a health centre formulates guidelines and criteria on the basis of available expertise and attempts consensus through discussions. If necessary, literature is studied or experts are consulted. Other parties may be involved as well. Advantages of this approach are that it is educational for the participants, that it increases their sense of commitment and 'ownership', and that the chance of acceptance is good (Table 2.2). A disadvantage is that the task is probably too difficult for the average GP, who lacks the necessary skills and expertise. In the North of England Study of Standards and Performance (1992) local, small groups of GPs, sometimes supported by a medical specialist, developed guidelines by means of a structured procedure for a series of topics in general practice care. The procedure included reading literature, collecting existing standards, developing branching logic skills, and group discussions. Each group developed its own guidelines and the results were shared with other groups in the region. The impact of some of the guidelines on practice health outcomes was evaluated. Improvements were found in the prescribing and follow-up behaviour of GPs and in the compliance and health status of the patients for some health problems.

Table 2.3   *A central versus a decentralized approach*

Approach	Advantage	Disadvantages
Decentralized (consensus in practice or local groups)	Educational Commitment of target group ('ownership') Guidelines adapted to local situation Acceptance/adoption may be easy	Time-consuming, difficult job Lack of specific expertise/skills No systematic analysis of literature Group processes important Average performance as guideline Different guidelines in same district
Central (consensus procedure on national/regional scale)	Sound scientific basis Structured, thorough procedure Broad professional basis Uniformity New insights/research Gives direction to CME* vocational training schemes Efficient approach	Time consuming, expensive Target group not involved, 'no ownership' Necessarily global Not adapted to specific needs and local situations Provokes fear, misunderstanding among GPs Potential abuse by 'outsiders' (government, funders, patients)

*CME = continuing medical education.

Developing guidelines in this way proved to be difficult and to demand interpersonal, technical, and clinical expertise.

A central approach

A group of expert GPs develops guidelines and criteria with a broad, preferably national or regional, legitimacy on the basis of a rigorous analysis of scientific literature and clinical experience. Advantages of this approach are its scientific basis and its contribution to more uniformity in general practice care. For the individual practitioner this may be a blessing, as it is becoming increasingly problematic to keep up with all new scientific developments. A potential problem, however, is that care providers may reject guidelines that they have not developed themselves. To a certain extent, people will always want to reinvent new products and adapt them to their own situation (Roger 1983).

Since 1989 the Dutch College of General Practitioners has been publishing national guidelines for general practice, developed by means of a very thorough procedure (Grol 1990a). An independent advisory board selects subjects suitable for standard setting. In 9 to 15 monthly sessions a working party of GPs, varying from those who are very well informed to those with a little more than average interest, draws up a draft. This process is supported by members of the college staff, who also do the editing. The draft is sent for comments to 50 GPs selected at random. Additional comments are obtained from relevant specialists. The revised draft is then assessed in an independent committee that scrutinizes the scientific justification

Table 2.4 *Opinion of GPs in The Netherlands on national standards for general practice care: percentage who totally agree (Grol 1992)*

	Feb. 1989 $n = 453$ (%)	Sept. 1990 $n = 339$ (%)
Are basis for daily work	82	82
Are important for getting a uniform policy among GPs	79	87
Make clear to 'outsiders' what general practice stands for	61	64
Should not become compulsory	56	62
Can be abused	22	33

Table 2.5 *Opinions of GPs in The Netherlands on the use of national guidelines: percentage saying very useful (Grol 1992)*

Useful for	%
Vocational training	85
Peer review	84
Continuing medical education	84
Arrangements with colleagues	81
Self-audit	73
Reaccreditation	39
Contracting or budgeting	25

of the guidelines. After approval, the guidelines are given a well-organized form and published in the scientific monthly journal for GPs. Evaluation of the acceptance of these national guidelines revealed a very positive attitude of practitioners to this initiative (Grol 1991; see for example Tables 2.4 and 2.5).

GUIDELINE DEVELOPMENT AT VARIOUS LEVELS

A synthesis between central and decentralized standard setting probably offers the best prospect for development and actual implementation of guidelines and criteria in practice and in quality improvement and peer review activities (Table 2.6). At a central level (national, regional) the scientific basis and a broad acceptance of the guideline are important. A rigorous, structured procedure is applied for this purpose (consensus conferences, Delphi methods, and other structured procedures). However, these guidelines are necessarily of a global nature. On a local and practice level (health centre, group practice, local group of GPs) specific guidelines and criteria should be developed in accordance with local need, on the basis of the available central guidelines. In this way, the processes of guideline development are complementary and mutually stimulating.

In Chapter 8 the methods for the development of specific criteria and targets for peer review are presented in more detail.

Table 2.6   *Development of practice guidelines and criteria at different levels*

Level	Aim	Who?	How?
National, regional	Scientific basis Broad acceptance in profession Accountability of general practice Give direction to CME* and QA†	Professional organizations Experts in general practice Representatives of other parties (patients, insurances)	Structured procedures Delphi procedures Consensus conferences
Local	Development of local guidelines Arrangements between GPs and other care providers	Groups of collaborating GPs Specialists, hospitals Other disciplines	Peer review Group consensus methods
Practice	Development of practice protocols and targets	GPs Other workers in the practice Patient representatives	Quality circles Structured discussions in practice meetings
Individual	Setting of individual objectives for quality improvement	GP Peers	Self-audit Peer review

*CME = continuing medical education; † = quality assurance.

3 Observing practice and evaluating care in peer review

INTRODUCTION

After setting criteria and target standards for evaluating general practice care the next steps in the peer review process are concerned with observing practice and collecting data on the actual care provided to patients. What kind of care is delivered and to what extent does it meet the quality criteria?

Assessing patient care is a crucial activity in quality improvement. Care providers often overestimate what they do. Providing information about what actually happens makes performance clear to doctors themselves, to their peers, and to others. In particular, it will stimulate a process of peer review enormously.

Without doubt, most general practitioners and other care providers in primary care do their utmost to offer good care to patients. For many years we have relied on vocational training and continuing medical education (CME) to guarantee competence. The difference with quality assurance is particularly in the collection of data on actual care and evaluating care against accepted criteria for good quality.

In this chapter a brief overview is presented of methods which are valid, reliable, feasible, and acceptable.

EVALUATING CARE

The evaluation of patient care for specific aspects of general practice with defined criteria consists of the following elements, which are sometimes a little difficult to separate:

1. Data collection: information is gathered on actual care related to the selected indicators.
2. Data analysis: the information is evaluated, comparing actual care with criteria for good quality, drawing conclusions on areas which need improvement.
3. Feedback: information on necessary improvement is given in a well-organized and understandable manner.

Data collection

Instruments and procedures for gathering information on patient care, which are feasible for peer review, need to fit well into normal family practice working routines (Difford 1990). Practice staff (for example, a practice nurse, clinical assistant, receptionist or a practice manager) can be involved in collecting data (Irvine

Table 3.1   *Methods for evaluation of structure, process, and outcome in general practice*

Method	Structure	Medical process	Interpersonal process	Outcome
Monitoring, self-recording	*	*		*
Computerized monitoring	*	*		*
Chart audit	*	*		*
Practice observation	*		*	
Audio/videotaped consultations		*	*	
Sitting-in in surgery		*	*	
Interview GP/staff	*			
Patient survey	*	*	*	*
Knowledge/skill tests		*	*	
Data from insurers		*		*
Data from hospitals, pharmacists, etc.		*		*

Table 3.2   *Methods for evaluating general practice care*

Method	Reliability	Validity	Feasibility	Acceptability
Monitoring, self-recording	+/–	+	++	++
Computerized monitoring	+/–	+	+	+
Chart audit	+	+/–	++	+
Practice visit, observation	+	+/–	+	+
Audio/videotape consultations	+/–	++	+/–	+/–
Sitting-in in surgery	+/–	++	+	–
Interview GP/staff	–	+	+	++
Patient survey	+	+/–	+/–	+/–
Knowledge/skill tests	+	–	+/–	+
Data from insurers	+/–	+/–	+	–
Data from hospitals, pharmacists, etc.	+/–	+/–	+	+

1991; Essex 1991; Baker and Presley 1990). There are many sources for collecting data: patients, GPs, practice staff, colleagues, hospital, pharmacy, insurers, etc.

Each aspect of care—structure, process, and outcome—calls for specific instruments and procedures for data collection (see Table 3.1). In the past most of the data collection methods for general practice have been developed for research purposes. However, these often do not fit well into systematic, regular, or continuous peer review or quality assurance processes. Data collection methods for peer review should be (Table 3.2):

• Valid: the data reflect the actual quality of care for a certain topic; this is achieved, on the one hand, by a good selection of crucial indicators, on the other by a method that really is able to measure what it should measure, for example it is very difficult to assess the communication with the patient by means of a chart audit.

- Realiable: the assessment is reproducible; if data collection is repeated the same results are achieved.
- Feasible: data collection is easy, can be managed in a simple way, and fits well into normal practice routines; there is a low investment of time, money, materials, and staff.
- Acceptable: the data collection method is acceptable to the doctors and practice staff; the aims are clear and acceptable, and the involved care providers are convinced that the data are handled carefully.

Data analysis

Analysing data involves comparing data on the actual performance of one GP or practice with data from other GPs and practices and with the criteria for good quality and coming to conclusions about strong points, gaps, and needs. This aspect of peer review is often seen as the most threatening by care providers, because it may involve criticism that is unpleasant. It may help to remember that people are making judgements all the time. It is a part of normal life. We appraise faces, words, motives, and behaviour of others, generally in an implicit and subjective way, unsupported by evidence. In the evaluation of data on patient care we can be more objective, in particular since explicit, accepted criteria are used and since conclusions on necessary improvements are grounded on evidence, on facts, on reliable and valid data from general practice.

The data are studied and compared with the criteria and targets. Data from other GPs, practice workers, and practices involved in the peer review process are also compared. Trends and patterns in performance and specific deficiencies and needs of the practice are noted. This can be done by the care provider, by an external assessor, or by a patient. In this book the emphasis is on evaluation by peers or colleagues.

Some data are suitable for computerization and can be collected in the course of day-to-day care and analysed with standard statistical procedures, before being used in a peer review activity. For other topics and methods person-to-person analysis and feedback are suitable, for example for the evaluation of consultations on audio- or videotape, sitting in the surgery, or observation of the practice premises.

Feedback

Feedback is perhaps the heart of the whole peer review exercise: 'The value of feedback in the modification of behaviour cannot be doubted. It is a fundamental biological process... it is the basis of all learning' (McIntyre and Popper 1983). A clear and understandable overview of the results of data analysis is given:

- in a written manner, for example in the form of tables or figures with trends, comparing data of a GP or practice with the criteria and/or with data from peers and other practices;
- in a personal manner, where a colleague gives comments on performance in a clear and positive way.

Good feedback gives an accurate picture and interpretation of the quality of care and is helpful and supportive to the doctors and the practice in improving care. It stimulates discussions, critical reflection, and intention to change. Feedback is the link between observation and implementation of change in general practice care.

EVALUATION PROCEDURES TO BE USED IN PEER REVIEW

Tables 3.1 and 3.2 have shown some evaluation methods for general practice with their strong and weak points and an indication of those aspects of care where their application is particularly suitable. A brief description of the various procedures is presented below and their feasibility for peer review is discussed.

Recording or monitoring

During or after contacts with patients the doctor or another practice worker fills in, on a structured checklist or form, which activities have been performed. This method is very practical and widely acceptable. Monitoring generally does not take much time if the form is well designed. However, there is a chance that the doctor over- or underestimates performance and that the data are not very reliable. The data can be summarized and used very easily for review and feedback in a peer group.

Computerized monitoring

The data can also be collected and analysed with the help of a computer. One method is to install a specific software programme for data analysis (for example, Epi-Info, a programme of the World Health Organization (WHO)). Newer developments allow the automated extraction of data from a computerized patient record. The great advantage of using the computer for data collection and evaluation is that it makes work much easier. Data stored during contacts with patients can later be collected and aggregated. In future such methods may be increasingly integrated with the automated patient record, though this may require a recording discipline which is not yet common among doctors. A print-out of the analysed data can be circulated among the members of a peer review group or a practice team for discussion.

Chart audit

A randomized sample of patient records is extracted and analysed by a peer or a practice assistant. The sample may be stratified (for example, men between 55 and 65 or patients with a certain chronic disease). Having an age/sex register and records marked for specific risk groups speeds up the selection of records enormously. Another approach is to bring some records to the peer review meeting, where colleagues study them and give feedback on the basis of this analysis. Chart audit is a feasible and acceptable method for quality assessment, which has been successfully used in several countries. However, its value depends heavily on the quality of record keeping. Because family doctors differ widely in recording data on their contacts with patients, important information can be lacking in the records and so the method has restricted validity. The audit may only reveal the quality of record keeping.

Practice observation

A visit to a general practice can be made to observe especially the structure and process of care. This can be done using checklists to compare findings against defined criteria in order to ensure that visitors make a thorough review. Examples of this are in the British Royal College's *Fellowship by assessment* (Royal College of General Practitioners 1990), the accreditation processes used for teachers in several countries, for example, New Zealand (Royal New Zealand College of General Practitioners 1990) and the Australian College's inter-practice visit process.

Audio- or videotaped consultations

Use of audio- or videotapes is an important tool for collecting data on the process of the consultation. If patients consent (preferably in writing), the doctor tapes 10–20 consultations. A selection is made afterwards and the consultations are assessed using specific guidelines. This method is particularly useful and feasible for reviewing doctor–patient communication, patient education, the counselling of patients, and the structure of the consultation. Observing consultations is important because they are at the heart of general/family medicine. Recording provides a rich source of data about the doctor's performance in this crucial activity. The tape can be played several times to arrive at a good assessment. However, the evaluation is subjective most of the time. Achieving a reliable judgement is sometimes difficult. At least 10 consultations are needed to arrive at generalizable results, which is a heavy investment of time and money.

Sitting in

A colleague sits in during consultations and collects data on performance in contacts with patients, preferably using structured checklists or observation sheets. This method is particularly useful for evaluating medical-technical skills (examinations and manual procedures) which are often not recorded on videotape. The observed doctor's performance will be affected to a certain extent—most doctors are not used to having an observer in their surgery.

Interviewing the general practitioner and staff

Data on organization of services and practice premises can be collected quickly by obtaining information from the doctor and the practice staff in a written questionnaire or a structured interview. The data can be used in peer group activities later on. Reliability may be a problem since doctors and staff may paint a more optimistic picture than actually exists.

Patient surveys

Patients receive a written questionnaire (or telephone or person-to-person interview) with questions on availability and quality of care and services. Or they may be given a questionnaire about their (functional) health status. Questionnaires can be sent to a sample of patients in the practice or handed out before or after a consultation. Specific patient groups can be selected for this purpose (for example, patients with chronic disease, parents of sick children). This is clearly a very relevant method. However, it is not yet clear which aspects of family practice care can properly and validly be assessed by patients. There is a well-known tendency for individuals to rate their own doctor highly, even when satisfaction with doctors in general may be considerably lower. However, much useful qualitative information is obtained. Valid and reliable instruments and procedures are now being developed in many countries.

Competency testing: knowledge and skills

Knowledge or decision-making skills can be assessed by means of written tests (multiple-choice questions, structured cases, etc.). The relationship between test scores and practice performance is generally not very strong or well established as yet. However, if the goal is to improve competence, then a well-designed knowledge test can be reliable tool, which is easy to administer and analyse. Another method uses a test situation, in which a GP's performance in practice is simulated. This is done by using trained simulated patients, who play a specific role to test examination, therapeutic, or communication skills. Models can be used to test specific technical skills (for example, the insertion of an intrauterine device or surgical skills). These types of competence testing may be built into a peer review process, when peers observe and criticize the performance of their colleague (for example, from behind a one-way screen).

Data from insurers, hospitals, pharmacists, etc.

In many countries data on prescription, referrals, and test ordering are collected by insurers or hospitals as a normal routine. These data can be a start for evaluating patient care among peers. However, the lack of information on the decision process which preceded the referral, prescription, or test ordering makes adequate interpretation of the findings difficult. This source of data can also be used for identifying general areas that need to be addressed in the peer review process.

CONCLUSION

Collecting and analysing data on patient care in general practice and giving understandable and well-organized feedback to colleagues and practices is an important step in a peer review process. The data may give a clear picture of the work of the practice for the GPs themselves, for practice staff, and possibly also for 'outsiders'.

Collecting data on individual and practice performance offers a sound basis for learning and improving with peers. Ideally this data collection is continuous and a normal part of the practice work. Simple, understandable methods are used and each practice worker is involved. In Part II we present a selection of methods that may be valuable in a continuous practice-based or local peer review process.

4 Improvement and change through peer review

'In my opinion, effectiveness in inducing behavioural change is the most important, yet least understood problem in quality monitoring today'.

(Donabedian 1986)

INTRODUCTION

Improving and changing practice performance is definitely the most complex step in medical audit. It is also an aspect which is often undervalued or neglected (Pringle *et al.* 1991). Nevertheless, there is a lot of evidence that, even if care providers are well informed about what they should be doing, they often do not perform in accordance with their knowledge or skills (Kosecoff *et al.* 1987; Sanazaro 1983), so behaviour change is desirable.

There are naive ideas about stimulating change in medical practice. The proposed strategies are often restricted to continuing medical education (CME) by means of lectures or group discussions. Research on CME usually shows that the effect on actual performance in practice is marginal (Lomas and Haynes 1988; Haynes *et al.* 1984; Stein 1981). One reason for the lack of effect of such approaches is that too little attention is given to the specific barriers to change in certain groups of physicians and practices and that there is little use as yet of interventions that are known to be effective in changing behaviour. A continuous peer review process may offer a very powerful stimulus in bringing about desirable changes in practice performance, provided that sufficient attention is given to it during the review activities. This implies that, after setting target standards, collecting and analysing data on actual care, and receiving feedback, the time has come for planning and implementing changes in practice routines.

CHANGE AS A STEPWISE PROCESS

In order to achieve change in practice performance several steps must be taken (McGuire 1981; Rogers 1983; Fishbein and Azjen 1975; Bandura 1986; Grol 1992a). General practitioners must:

- be informed and interested in the expected practice performance;
- be informed on and aware of specific deficiencies in the current practice performance;
- have a positive attitude to the expected practice performance;

- have a willingness and intention to change and confidence in the success of it;
- be prepared to implement changes in practice;
- maintain change and recognize positive outcomes.

At each step various factors are related to successful outcome and specific problems and barriers might inhibit progress (Table 4.1). It is important to identify and be aware of these factors and barriers, to discuss them during peer review, and to adapt specific actions to them (Grol 1992*a*).

Barriers in the care provider

Competence

The care provider lacks the necessary knowledge or skills to perform the expected behaviour; may not have the opportunity to experiment with the new performance; or may underestimate the deficiencies in the provided care.

Motivation, attitude

The care provider sees more disadvantages than advantages or may expect negative consequences of the proposed changes; may not view the changes as feasible or applicable in the situation or not see any possibility of implementing them in practice; they may also not fit into the care provider's existing opinions and values with regard to work.

Table 4.1   *Barriers in the process of improvement and change*

Steps in the change process	Possible problems/barriers
1. Interest, commitment	No needs or interest
	No reading/selective reading
	No contact with colleagues
2. Insight	Insufficient knowledge or skills
	No awareness of gaps in own routines
	Overestimation of own performance
3. Acceptance	Seeing more disadvantages than advantages
	Not feeling involved, committed
	Expecting problems, negative consequences
	Negative attitude of opinion leaders in network
	Change requires extra time/money
4. Change	Seeing no concrete alternatives
	Inadequate practice premises
	No confidence in success
	Forgetting, reverting to old routines
	Negative outcomes of change, no reinforcement

Table 4.2 *Problems experienced by GPs in complying with national guidelines for the management of a sprained ankle (n = 320)*

This is a problem	% agree
Patients often go directly to the hospital	83
Patients have doubts about the competence of the GP with regard to this problem	60
GP does not have the bandaging skills	54
Physiotherapists take over the treatment	53
Insufficient research available for this subject	36
Extra workload on weekend services in general practice	28
Insufficient knowledge of the condition	24

Personal characteristics

The care provider may lack the confidence that the expected changes can be implemented adequately, or may be someone who is generally conservative and not inclined to take risks, to change, or to adopt new approaches.

Barriers in the setting

Social factors

Other care providers, specialists, persons in the network of the care provider, and also patients may have different opinions on the proposed change and refuse to co-operate.

Structural, logistic, and organizational factors

The prerequisites for change may not be available in the practice or the work setting, or the change may demand an extra investment of time or money. The proposed change may interfere with existing practice routines or require alterations in practice management. Finally, local or regional infrastructures, rules, or laws may interfere with the change.

Each of these barriers may play a part in preventing necessary improvements in general practice care through a peer review process. Interventions and actions should be focused on these barriers. For example, a survey among a randomized sample of Dutch GPs with regard to their problems with national guidelines for a sprained ankle disclosed that, in particular, barriers related to the network of the GP seemed to inhibit change in practice (Table 4.2). Most of the respondents saw the attitude of the patients in this case as a problem, as well as the role of the hospital emergency departments and the physiotherapists. Strategies for inducing changes should, therefore, be aimed primarily at educating patients and negotiating the mutual responsibilities of GPs and specialists (Grol 1992*a*).

EFFECTIVE METHODS FOR INDUCING CHANGES

There is not an ideal strategy or intervention for changing practice performance. Many different factors and barriers operate, doctors and practices differ in experiences, needs, and learning styles. So a variety of methods is generally required to bring about lasting changes:

- Intensive, long-lasting interventions, in which the 'message' is repeated again and again, are necessary (Lomas and Haynes 1988; Haynes and Davies 1984; Eisenberg 1985; Spoxy *et al.* 1989).
- It may require written as well as personal approaches, use of mass-media as well as small group and individually directed approaches; and interventions aimed at knowledge, skills, and attitudes as well as those addressing performance and behaviour (Soumerai *et al.* 1990; Winkler *et al.* 1985).
- These interventions should be directed towards existing barriers and problems in bringing about change (Fineberg 1985; Flora and Farquhar 1988).

Methods for implementing changes in practice might range from predominantly facilitating and educational approaches to more coercive approaches. Their effectives varies (Table 4.3).

AWARENESS AND CHANGE THROUGH PEER REVIEW

In our experience care providers undergo an educational process whilst taking part in peer review, in that they take on a self-critical stance with regard to their profession and their own performance. The peer review is directed towards achieving a more self-conscious, more rational, and more self-critical approach. The process of

Table 4.3 *Effectiveness of various interventions and strategies for implementing changes*

Interventions and Strategies	Effectiveness
Facilitating, educational methods	
Mailed educational materials	–
CME, courses, group education	+/–
Face-to-face, individual instruction	+
Audit and feedback	+/–
Peer review, practice visits	+
Coercive, controlling methods	
Structural arrangements (provisions, staff)	?
Incentives, sanctions, barriers to performance	+/–
Regulations, laws, certification, contracts	?

awareness begins when a care provider is in a situation, possibly with the aid of colleagues, of comparing his/her own performance with the explicit criteria of adequate general practice care.

This activity may result in two different situations (Sheldon 1982):

- The carer's own (practice) performance appears to tally with the standards of good quality. Some participants treat this as quite normal and only to be expected and do not reflect upon the result for any length of time. For others it may have the effect of making them aware of their strong points which gives them a boost of self-confidence. It will motivate them to continue with the peer review.
- The carer's (practice) performance does not comply with the defined targets. When this happens a complex chain reaction is sparked off which leads to negative and positive reactions, which may prove either beneficial or detrimental for the learning process. We have attempted to show this process in a general schematic way (Fig. 4.1) and the following gives a description of it.

Tension may arise when it becomes clear that the carer's (practice) performance differs from that of colleagues' and when criticism is given. The general practitioner audited might already be aware of the discrepancy, but on the other hand it might mean that previously held self-esteem is marred: self-perception as a health professional, the way the practitioner felt about his/her capability and performance is suddenly disturbed. In the literature this is referred to as 'cognitive dissonance'. It is worth noting that a state of dissonance motivates people to remove the dissonance as quickly as possible, by adapting their self-view to the new information or by going on the defensive. As a result, in peer review, one can make a distinction between the different reactions which are evoked due to criticism and interference with self-image.

Acceptance of the criticism

The criticism is labelled as useful and as something from which one will benefit. The criticism and the underlying criteria are critically weighed up and the valuable elements are absorbed. They become inner criteria, a sort of 'conscience'. ('I catch myself diverging from the criterion frequently during consultations'). If this happens we are dealing with active acceptance. On the other side there is passive acceptance: the criticism is accepted, it is seen as true, but does not lead to changes being made. There is a chance that the criticism will be labelled as not useful and treated like bad news. This instigates frustration rather than willingness to change ('Following the criteria has led to longer working hours. My consultation session runs behind schedule more often, which I do not like at all').

Dismissal of the criticism

Criticism is ignored, either consciously or unconsciously, or a clearly defensive reaction is evoked, which usually takes one of the following forms:

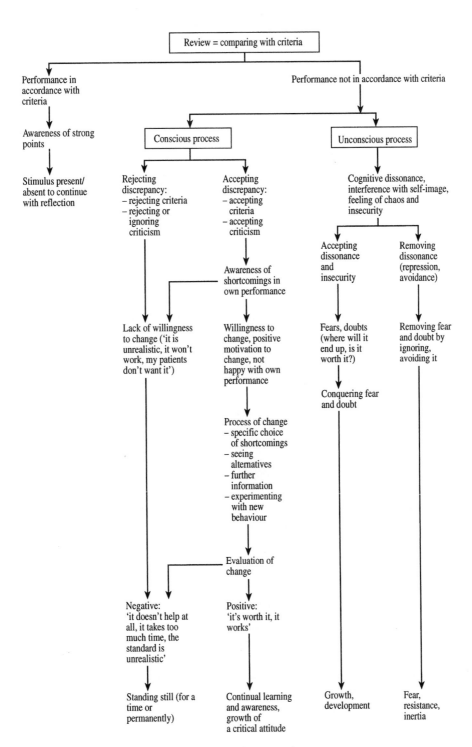

Fig. 4.1   The learning and awareness process in peer review.

- Refuting the criticism: the criticism is said not to be relevant on the basis of things like exceptional circumstances: 'I usually act differently, it is due to the patient, I know this particular patient,' and so forth.
- Reject the criteria: 'the criteria are not realistic, in practice things work quite differently, it is asking too much, what it boils down to is that the patient should feel satisfied, there is no guarantee that things will be better if I do it differently,' and so forth.

For true awareness of the situation the practice workers must accept the criticism: 'this applies to me, to us, to our practice'.

CHANGE THROUGH PEER REVIEW

Changes are generally made with the greatest of effort. People have often been working in a certain way for years, and are quite happy with the results; and in some ways quite rightly so. Even if one is not pleased with one's own style, efforts to do things differently are not always a great success. Changing the established shortcomings demands energy and perseverance, whilst the results are by no means guaranteed. There is a danger that the practice will be thrown into a commotion for a while or that patients will not benefit from the change or will not be understanding. No one can say whether the pleasure and satisfaction which one gains from one's work will be increased or maintained by trying new methods. Better the devil you know than the devil you don't know.

Change for some people means pleasant excitement, a feeling of adventure, and new energy. For others it is more a case of anxiety ('What is going to happen to me, will I stay the same person, will I lose control?') and doubt ('What will I gain from it, is it worth putting so much time and energy into it?'). For yet another group, it represents an unwelcome interruption in their set pattern and rhythm of life and work. The change may ask for considerable investment of time, energy, or even money to solve all kinds of structural, social, or organizational problems. It is a weighing up of these sort of attractive and unattractive aspects of change which will decide whether one is willing to work at improving one's performance, or whether one concludes that it is better not to embark on this course at all (using the arguments: 'it isn't feasible, my patients aren't used to it, it'll take too much time, if I do it another way it won't be me anymore,' and so forth).

In our experience of peer review, the process of change takes place in a number of definite steps:

- awareness of specific shortcomings in one's performance as a GP or in the care provision process of the practice;
- a nagging feeling about these shortcomings; this is decisive for the willingness to correct practice behaviour; recognizing the same problem in colleagues usually plays an important role in this;
- insight in the causes of these shortcomings and in possible barriers to change;

- awareness of possible alternative practice behaviour; seeing how colleagues work and change can be an important influence in this, as well as support and some pressure from peers;
- acquiring further information or advice (through colleagues or study) on a different approach; solving practical or structural problems;
- actively experimenting with different behaviour in practice and evaluating its result;
- incorporating the change in the practice routines; adoption of the change by all involved.

CONCLUSIONS

The most complex step in a peer review process is actually changing practice performance, when necessary. Various steps have to be taken in order to stimulate necessary changes:

- identifying specific areas for change;
- identifying specific barriers to achieving these changes; these can be factors related to the care providers or social, structural, or organizational factors;
- planning and implementing the changes with support of peers.

It is particularly relevant to emphasize the implementation of desirable changes during peer review. At a certain stage every participant experiences the need to evaluate to what extent taking part in peer review has led to improvements. This is, implicitly, a cost-benefit analysis: 'Have we achieved what we had in mind? Is it worth doing and worth pursuing?' If the question can be answered in the affirmative, it will be a spur for further audit. If, on the other hand, no real improvement in the care for patients have been shown, these questions will be answered in the negative: 'It will never work, it takes up too much time, let's do something else for a change.' Thus, although it is the most difficult step, achieving improvements is the driving force for a continuous peer review process.

5 Effects of peer review: the evidence

INTRODUCTION

What is the evidence from the literature concerning audit, feedback, and peer review? Do these really have any impact on the quality of care in medical practice and on the performance of care providers? In this chapter a brief overview is presented of available studies in this area. One project is presented as an example of a continuous peer review process: 'Peer review in The Netherlands'.

AUDIT AND FEEDBACK

Many studies concerning the effects of audit and feedback on performance have yielded positive results (for example Nelson 1976; Frame *et al.* 1984; Fleming & Lawrence 1983; Berwick 1986, Fowkes *et al.* 1986; Winkens *et al.* 1992). Rosser (1983), for instance, asked 30 general practitioners to estimate how much diazepam they prescribed and provided them subsequently with feedback and actual figures. This led to a decrease in the number of prescriptions. Audit of patients' records and feedback on test ordering resulted in a change in perform-ance (Martin *et al.* 1980). In a further study doctors developed criteria for the ade-quate management of cystitis and vaginitis and after performance they got feedback. This led to an increase in following the criteria (Norton and Dempsey 1985). Gehlbach *et al.* (1984) provided physicians with feedback on prescribing and with information on alternative and less expensive solutions. The experimen-tal group in this controlled study had an increase of 46 per cent in prescribing the recommended medication.

Various studies point to the importance of 'individualized feedback', that is feed-back focused on the behaviour of the individual care providers. Winnickoff (1984) compared three approaches aimed at improving the screening for colon carcinoma, namely continuing medical education (CME), group feedback, and individual feed-back. The last intervention yielded the greatest effect. According to the authors this was partly due to the subjects wishing to perform as well as or better than their colleagues. Most people dislike achieving less well than those to whom they compare themselves. Sommers *et al.* (1984) compared the effects of formulating criteria as a group with mutual discussion of audit results and individual feedback. Individual feedback turned out most effective. Personal, individualized feedback reports on test ordering by a respected specialist, with information on the volume and the quality of the decisions made by GPs, resulted in a very considerable reduction in test ordering (Winkens *et al.* 1992).

Audit and feedback may be influential. However, there are also doubts on their effects. The results seem to be less positive when the feedback is not provided regularly or maintained for a protracted period (Fowkes 1982). In some study no effects were found (Grivell *et al.* 1981; Schroeder *et al.* 1984; Wones 1987; Parrino 1989). Feedback on the costs of laboratory use in a controlled study did not have any effect on behaviour (Cohen *et al.* 1982). Everett *et al.* (1983) examined the costs of test ordering and compared feedback alone with chart audit, feedback, and group discussions about performance. The first method did not lead to changes, the second one was more successful. Summarizing the literature on audit and feedback one can state that these are particularly effective

- if the feedback is personal, individualized;
- if it is continued over a protracted period;
- if it is given by respected colleagues;
- if the audit and feedback are part of a more comprehensive peer review process.

PEER REVIEW

Receiving criticism of colleagues within the setting of a small, safe group seems especially promising (Eisenberg 1985; Grol 1990*b*). For example, Post (1984) examined the effects on prescribing behaviour of holding discussions between GPs and pharmacists. Guidelines were formulated for prescribing antibiotics and subsequently performance was discussed by means of feedback on prescription data. This led to a fall in the number of prescriptions. Peer review of consultation skills using audio- or videotapes has also been shown to affect practice performance (Verby *et al.* 1979; Grol *et al.* 1988*b*).

The introduction of peer review seems to be particularly successful when it is used as part of a wider approach in which different methods and interventions, aimed at influencing behaviour, are combined (Lomas and Haynes 1988). Klein *et al.* (1981), for instance, examined the effects of an extensive intervention on the prescription of antibiotics in uncomplicated cases of urinary tract infection. First, inadequate routines and gaps in knowledge and skills were identified by audit. Next, various relevant educational activities were organized. A significant change in prescribing ensued. Frame *et al.* (1989) employed various interventions in their study (audit of the medical records of patients, feedback on deficiencies in performance, group discussions). Modifications of the provided care resulted, although it was not clear which intervention had the greatest impact.

In some studies an emphasis on certain activities in the peer review process proved to be influential, for example emphasis on setting guidelines by a peer group (Fowkes 1986; Grant *et al.* 1985; North of England Study 1992) or on exchanging practice routines (Birmingham Research Unit 1977). Generally, however, a combination of activities is most effective. Putnam and Curry (1980), for instance, carried out an effective programme in which physicians first developed criteria in a peer group. Next, performance was assessed on the basis of chart review and finally an educational programme was offered, directed to the gaps and needs of the group. Palmer *et al.* (1985) had a comparable programme, in which the participants went through the peer review cycle several times with success.

Finally, in the peer review project of the University of Nijmegen (Grol *et al.* 1988*a* and *b*), from which many of the ideas described in this book are derived, different methods were combined: the introduction of guidelines for adequate care, training in various audit skills, peer review, and skills training. Alterations occurred in the consultation process as well as in the history taking, the giving of advice and guidance, and the prescribing behaviour by GPs (see example).

The line of thought in these studies is that insight into one's own performance through audit and peer review in a safe group of respected colleagues can be an important instrument with regard to change and to improvement of the quality of general practice care.

Example: 'Peer review in The Netherlands' (Grol *et al.* 1988*a*, Grol 1990*b*)

In the beginning of the 1980s a large experiment in the eastern part of The Netherlands was carried out in which a comprehensive peer review methodology was developed. GPs took part in groups of 10 persons, which met once a month over a long period (average 1.5 years). In the course of this programme the GPs developed a positive attitude towards quality assurance and peer review and acquired the necessary skills for it. They also gained some experience with various evaluation procedures: self-monitoring their performance with checklists, audiotaped consultations, and mutual practice observation and sitting in the surgery. The participants evaluated the programme very positively. More than 90 per cent thought that participation was very valuable for their daily work; 60 per cent were of the opinion that the peer review had increased the joy and satisfaction of working as a GP and 40 per cent maintained that participation had given them a new basis for their work. Only 5 per cent said that the peer review did not contribute to their practice work. The actual changes in performance were assessed in a group of 43 participants by means of measurement in practice before and after the programme. A significant improvement was found for history taking, patient education, and prescribing of medication (50 per cent of the participants showed an increase of more than 5 per cent on following criteria for adequate clinical performance; about one-third an increase of more than 10 per cent for communicating with patients; an increase of more than 10 per cent on following the criteria was seen in an average 50–70 per cent of the participants). It was estimated that the cost of prescribing was reduced by approximately £2000 a year for an average practice.

The participants were asked to describe which factors were most influential in encouraging changes in performance (Table 5.1). It was reported that, in particular, exchanging practice experiences with colleagues, becoming aware of gaps in one's own performance, and being aware of new practice guidelines were particularly significant with regard to stimulating change.

On the basis of experiences with peer review among GPs, the professional organizations for GPs in The Netherlands have decided that participation in peer review in local groups will be compulsory for all Dutch GPs in the near future. In order to achieve this objective, local GP representatives are being trained. They will be responsible for stimulating and supervising peer review in local groups and have to act as intermediaries in the dissemination of new guidelines and evaluation methods that can be used in the groups.

The training consists of three sessions of six hours in which the GPs learn about:

- chairing and supervising a group;
- setting up a comprehensive peer review programme;
- specific methods and tools to be used in the peer review process.

After having started peer review in their own local groups the GPs meet from time to time to exchange problems and experiences.

The participants in 15 of these groups were asked about their opinions with regard to the effectiveness of various common approaches to CME. Most of the GPs had experience with all these methods. The answers showed that continuous peer review in small groups was seen by these GPs as much more effective in many respects than the other methods (Table 5.2).

Table 5.1 *Factors in the peer review which are most influential in stimulating change (n = 131, percentages)*

Exchanging practice experiences with colleagues	25%
Awareness of gaps in performance	24%
Being aware of new guidelines	21%
Learning how to evaluate performance systematically	9%
Discovering that colleagues have failings too	7%
Learning about feasible practice routines of colleagues	7%
Other	7%
Total	100%

CONCLUSIONS

Review of the literature on the effectiveness of audit, feedback, and peer review disclosed that personal feedback, given over a protracted period by respected colleagues and which is part of more comprehensive peer review process, is effective. A combination of activities, evaluative as well as educational, should be included in this process.

Table 5.2   *Opinions of GPs on the effectiveness of various methods of continuing medical education (CME) (n = 140)*

	Method is very effective			
Aim	Peer review in small group (%)	Local CME meeting (%)	National regional CME course (%)	Hospital meeting (%)
Awareness of own performance	63	12	6	4
Becoming involved in CME	60	16	5	9
Changing performance	58	11	6	7
Complying with guidelines	56	10	4	6
Improving knowledge and skills	44	21	4	3

6 Conditions for the running of peer review groups

INTRODUCTION

In order to start peer review successfully and to run it smoothly, it is not enough to have a good programme, acceptable guidelines, and feasible evaluation tools. Certain conditions should be fulfilled to make the peer review process into a fruitful and valuable experience for the participants. These conditions are concerned with

- preparing the participants;
- characteristics of the peer groups;
- structural and organizational prerequisites;

PREPARING THE PARTICIPANTS

Research has indicated that general practitioners and practices are on the one hand motivated and on the other hand hesitant to partake in peer review on several grounds (Grol 1987). On the whole, care providers in general practice work on their own and are accountable only partly to others. This was largely the case in British general practice until recently, although the recent emphasis on audit has made peer review within group practice much more common. Participation in peer review gives colleagues the opportunity to take a peep behind the curtains and to offer their criticism. It goes without saying, that this may evoke fear and resistance. Participants may be frightened of being made a fool of in front of others, frightened that weak points will be brought to light, or that they will be branded as bad GPs. Or they may be convinced that no forms of criticism can ever take place objectively and fairly. In some cases, there may be a certain reluctance when it comes to criticizing others. They may have difficulty in accepting the criteria set up for adequate general practice care. This might mean that they feel they have to live up to an (unattainable) ideal. They may be frightened of becoming 'conveyor-belt products', or worried about being assessed on the basis of criteria which have been formulated by others. Many will not willingly give up their clinical freedom of approach in managing complaints and illness. Reasons for positive and negative reactions to peer review are given in Table 6.1 and 6.2.

There may also be uncertainty about the effect of the audit, whether participation will lead to results, or whether it will be worthwhile. They may be frightened that they will lose pleasure in their work. Apart from this, one finds that participants sometimes introduce all kinds of practical and financial objections ('takes a lot of time', 'difficult to organize') which may partly be the result of a certain amount of resistance.

Table 6.1   *Reasons for participating in peer review (n = 131, Grol 1987)*

	Very important reason (%)
I hope to identify gaps in my performance	94
I hope to correct gaps in my performance	90
I hope to learn how to communicate better with my patients	74
I want to learn about new developments in general practice	64
I want to learn more about myself as a GP	52
I am curious about peer review	51
I hope that peer review gives me more and better contacts with my colleagues	15
Peer review will possibly be compulsory in the future	8

Table 6.2   *Problems GPs have with taking part in peer review (n = 131, Grol 1987)*

	Very much a problem (%)
The investment of time	30
Being assessed and getting criticism	29
The fact that my performance will be related to an 'ideal' or 'norm'	19
Practical arrangements that have to be made	19
Giving comments on the performance of my peers	14
I do not see the need of peer review	1

RECRUITING AND MOTIVATING GENERAL PRACTITIONERS AND PRACTICES

All these objections and fears should be taken into account when peer activities are promoted. A thorough preparation and adequate motivation of GPs and practices is necessary.

In the Dutch peer review project (Grol *et al.* 1988*a*; Grol 1990) a start was made with the most motivated GPs in the district. They gained some experience with the peer review process. New groups were recruited by sending written invitations and by telephoning them. When they showed some interest, they were invited to a meeting where more information on the whole programme was given. Participants in the first group brought their experiences and answered questions. In this manner about 300 GPs from the district were motivated to take part in peer review groups.

A comparable approach was used by Boland in Ireland (personal report). In order to introduce a new, possibly threatening peer-review-based continuing education activity in the district, he first visited all key persons and opinion leaders. He discussed their problems and needs with regard to their work and to education and motivated them to take part in an experimental group. After having experienced this methodology they took over and started new groups. They succeeded in recruiting 90 per cent of the GPs in the district.

In motivating the GPs and practices to take part actively in the peer review it is important to emphasize the benefits they may gain from participation:

- better and more effective patient care;
- more awareness of their own performance and needs;
- more information on how to tackle certain problems in the practice;
- more and better contact with colleagues;
- better accountability to others—authorities, professionals, and patients;
- personal learning and improvement by peer review.

BASIC SKILLS

In order to profit optimally from the peer review, a number of basic skills must first be acquired. This need not occur separately from the actual peer review. In the initial phase a period may be included during which the emphasis lies on getting accustomed to the new activities and becoming familiar with the required skills. Some of these skills are:

- working constructively as a group;
- developing guidelines for care and criteria for evaluation;
- handling guidelines and criteria in peer review;
- designing or employing methods or instruments for gathering information on actual care;
- being able to receive criticism, overcoming fear of criticism;
- being able to give constructive criticism;
- formulating objectives for changing practice;
- supporting each other to achieve these objectives.

CHARACTERISTICS OF THE PEER REVIEW GROUP

The collaboration with colleagues is one of the most motivating and gratifying aspects of peer review. To get a good atmosphere in the group one needs:

- mutual confidence and respect among the group members;
- interest in each other's style of work;
- identification with one another, a common goal;
- sufficient diversity in practice experience;
- positive motivation with regard to peer review;
- absence of problems and tensions in mutual relationships;
- not too large a group (7–12 participants);
- readiness of all participants to meet regularly (at least once a month).

SUPERVISION

From experience with peer review thus far it has become clear that certain guidance for the peer review group is important, especially in the beginning. A supervisor must be capable of the following tasks:

- to pay attention to the functioning of the group; to establish an open and constructive atmosphere; to set an example by assuming a vulnerable position; to establish a clear structure, chairmanship, organization, etc;
- to pay attention to fears and aversions in the participants; to take these seriously, to admit and revisit them regularly; to offer the participants sufficient time to become accustomed to peer review; to safeguard the way criticism is given; to secure an atmosphere of a commitment, etc.
- to offer insight into the programme; to develop the handling of guidelines and methods of peer review; to teach basic skills, etc.

In the next part of the book, Chapter 8 is devoted to the supervision of peer review groups.

STRUCTURAL AND ORGANIZATIONAL CONDITIONS

Although it may appear trivial, a number of organizational aspects of peer review may well determine whether or not the peer review will succeed. Thus, among other things, the following should be taken heed of:

- long-term planning of meetings so that the participants will rarely be absent;
- continuity of peer review activities; at least one meeting every month is essential;
- clear agreements on what will be expected of each participant at the next meeting;
- a report in which the agreements are recorded and which reaches participants in good time;
- an appropriate location that permits undisturbed working;
- audiovisual and other facilities (blackboard, flip-chart, etc.);
- sufficient time for informal contacts (lunch, coffee).

In order to organize peer review for care providers in general practice group practices and health centres properly, the following structural conditions are required:

- sufficient time for all participants to meet and to prepare for meeting (about three to four hours per month);
- arrangements in the practice in order to achieve regular meetings and to guarantee data collections and analysis (who is on duty during meetings, who is responsible for collecting data, for evaluation of care and for feedback to the participants);
- supportive local, regional or national structures and regulations, e.g.
    - available guidelines and simple evaluation tools, which have been tested rigorously in practice; this will make life for the participants more simple;

– support in setting up these groups, advice on how to proceed; specially trained audit or quality assurance 'facilitators' may be available for this purpose;
– recognition for being involved in peer review: reimbursement of some of the costs involved and credit points for continuing medical education (CME) are incentives which will make peer review more attractive.

Part II

Methods of peer review

In the discovery of imperfection lies the chance for processes to improve.

Berwick (1989)

7 Methods for observing and reviewing practice with peers: some principles

INTRODUCTION

In this part of the book the development of performance review with peers and colleagues in a practice or in a local or regional group is taken a step further. In this chapter the model for peer review, presented in Chapter 1, is made more explicit and general principles of the peer review process are described. In the remaining chapters of this part of the book some methods of peer review process are described.

Peer review can be carried out between:

- two general practitioners (GPs);
- a group of care providers (GPs, practice nurses, midwives, community nurses, etc.) working in a group practice or a health centre;
- a group of GP locums;
- a regional continuing medical education (CME) group of GPs or care providers;
- a group of trainers or trainees in vocational training for general practice.

Let us assume that these persons are motivated to a certain degree and want to make a start with peer review, that is with observing and assessing each other's work, directly or indirectly. They agree to be involved in the peer review process for a certain period, for instance a year, and to meet each other regularly, say each month.

A PEER REVIEW PROCESS

Figure 1.1 represented a stepwise model for peer review, and various aspects of the process were described in Chapters 1–6. In practice, a whole series of distinct steps and activities have to be taken to perform peer review effectively:

Preparing for peer review
- acquiring peer review skills and becoming acquainted with the process;
- making arrangements for the practical and organizational aspects of peer review;
- formulating an explicit plan for six months or a year.

Selecting a suitable topic
- identifying relevant problems in individual or practice care;
- discussing and selecting topics for peer review;
- precisely defining these topics, restricting them to important issues.

Selecting and agreeing criteria and objectives

- agreeing on general goals for improving practice in relation to the selected topics;
- selecting the crucial indicators for the selected topics;
- defining the criteria for desirable performance;
- possibly, defining the specific target standards that a group or a practice wants to achieve.

Observing practice and evaluating care

- selecting or developing instruments and procedures for data collection and analysis;
- collecting data on practice performance;
- analysing these data: comparing performance with targets, looking at comparison with colleagues and at trends;
- giving understandable and well-organized feedback.

Planning and implementing changes

- identifying areas for change; selecting individual and practice goals for improvement;
- identifying specific problems and barriers to achieving these improvements;
- planning actions and selecting strategies to implement changes and solve the problems;
- carrying out the plan for change.

Follow-up

- analysing:
  - did the participants succeed?
  - if not, why not?
- planning for the repeat of certain steps.

This process is of a cyclic nature (Fig. 7.1). The steps do not have to start at any particular point. For instance rather than beginning by setting targets it can sometimes be wiser to start, after having selected a topic, with collecting and analysing data. These data can then be used to study the problems in practice and to agree on specific targets for improvement. Often it is best to work on several topics together so that once a project enters the 'analysis' and 'change' phase data collection can begin on the next topic.

Most care providers in general practice are under a constant pressure of time and are used to working fast. They tend to get easily bored if they address one particular topic for a very long time or apply one specific review method again and again. Experience has taught us the importance of continually varying both topics studied and methods used in peer review.

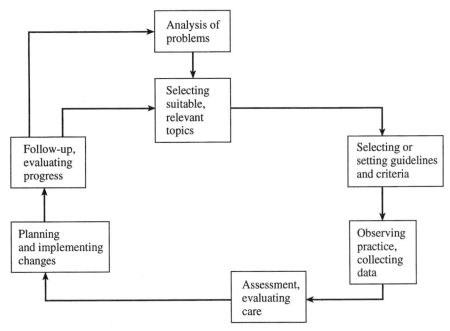

Fig. 7.1 The process of quality improvement by peer review (after Ovretveit 1992, Lawrence 1993, WHO 1993, *et al.*).

The various steps in the peer review process are discussed in more detail

PREPARATION

In order to be well prepared for peer review activities certain conditions are important:

- Mutual trust and respect, interest in each other's way of working, a sufficient level of motivation, and absence of problems and tensions among the group members. These items were highlighted in Chapter 6.
- Participants need to be educated in the methods of peer review. They should know how to select criteria, collect and analyse data, criticize each other, receive feedback, make a plan for change, and support each other in achieving these changes. Most care providers lack the experience and skills to manage these tasks well. Therefore, peer review should begin with one or more preparatory meetings in which the different activities are practised in an unthreatening fashion. Very simple topics are used to demonstrate the process. For this purpose, paper and pencil methods may be used (see examples). Also, data from practitioners or practices who are participating can be used as examples, which reduces threat in the early stages of learning. Reading specific parts and chapters from this book before the meetings may also be helpful.

Example: check-up oral contraception

Case: A young healthy woman (28 years) is visiting the GP. She has used the
    contraceptive pill for the past five years. She does not smoke. At previous
    check-ups no complaints were presented or problems found.
Question: What is the common routine in your practice with regard to the
    management of such a visit (examinations, advice, follow-up arrange-
    ments, personnel involved)?
Peer review process
- Participants write down their own procedure.
- In a plenary round the participants in turn present their current routines.
- Differences in routine are emphasized; 'is the variation in performance
  acceptable, rational?'
- Available standards or guidelines are introduced (e.g. a Dutch standard
  which says that in general check-ups for the contraceptive pill are unnecessary unless there are specific complaints and that a practice assistant
  can do the patient education and the management of the medication) and
  discussed; the group tries to achieve consensus on a common policy.
- Participants each determine what they should change in their routine to
  work up to the agreed policy and what kind of barriers there are in implementing the change.
- The group discusses the changes and the barriers to change; the participants help each other to find solutions, to offer alternative routines, etc.

- Arrangements have to be made on practical and organizational aspects of the
  peer review.
  - This should be done at the first meeting to ensure an efficient and attractive
    structure for the future meetings.
  - Arrangements must be made for when and where the group will meet.
    Meetings should take place in a task-oriented surrounding; peer review is a
    serious task, it is part of and not a relaxation from work.
  - Agreement on the length of the meetings. Generally, a meeting of a mini-
    mum of two hours or a maximum of three hours (with a short break of 10–15
    minutes) will be fine. A meeting of a whole day from time to time has the
    advantage of being away from practice and thus making optimal use of avail-
    able time. However, this will be difficult to plan on a regular basis for some
    GPs and practices.
  - One member of the group should be responsible for organizing the meetings
    and for taking care that specific prerequisites are available (video or audio
    equipment, flip-chart, materials for data collection, coffee or tea).
  - Some supervision for the group and the peer review process may be desir-
    able, especially in the beginning. This might be an external person or one

member of the group who has particular skills in chairing and supervising the process. The tasks of the supervisor will be described in Chapter 13.

- A plan for the meetings must be made and tasks shared. Ideally, a plan for a series of peer review sessions is made, say for 6–10 sessions over half a year or a year (see Table 7.1). This should include identification of who is responsible for data collection, analysis, literature analysis, report of the meeting, etc. Everyone should be well informed about what is to be done at any particular time. The arrangements and the plan should be recorded in the *meeting report*. The task of making and distributing such a report will be divided between the participants.

SELECTING A TOPIC, STATING PRIORITIES

The field of work in general practice is so broad and detailed and there are so many interesting topics, that a selection has to be made. It is impossible to address every-thing. For an ongoing group of care providers, involved in a continuous peer review and quality improvement process, it is recommended that topics are selected which are related to various structure, process, and outcome aspects of general practice. A frame-work for selecting topics is presented in Table 7.2 where a practical distinction has been made between clinical performance, general consultation skills, and practice management. It is recommended to select topics from each section of this framework in turn. In selecting a suitable topic various criteria may play a role (Irvine, 1991):

- The topic should be relevant and important in general practice care.
- It should occur frequently or involve a large proportion of daily work.
- There should be a recognized need for improvement in practice.
- New information or guidelines should have been published on the topic, which may make established routines old-fashioned or obsolete.

Table 7.1 *Example of a year programme for peer review of various topics (1, 2 and 3)*

	Session										Specific tasks
	1	2	3	4	5	6	7	8	9	10	
Preparing	*	*	*								
Selecting a topic	(1)			(2)			(3)				
Selecting or agreeing on criteria	(1)	(1)			(2)		(3)				
Observing practice, evaluating care		(1)	(1)		(2)	(2)		(3)			
Planning and implementing change			(1)	(1)		(2)		(3)	(3)		
Evaluation and follow-up					(1)		(2)			(1) (2) (3)	

Table 7.2   *A framework for selecting topics for peer review*

Aspects	Evaluation methods
Clinical performance	
History	Self-monitoring
Examinations, tests	Computerized monitoring
Prescribing	Chart review
Referring	Data from hospitals, pharmacists
Educating patients	Data from insurers
Counselling	Sitting in surgery
Prevention	Patient surveys
Individual	
Risk groups	
General consultation skills	
Structuring the care provision process	Audio/videotapes
Managing the relation with the patient	Sitting in surgery
Informing and instructing patients	Patient surveys
Practice management	
Equipment	Monitoring performance
Collaboration	Chart review
Within the practice	Practice observation
Outside the practice	Interview GP/staff
Organization of services	Patient surveys
Recording	
Medical	
Financial	
Organization of quality assurance	
Time-management	

- Desirable outcomes for the topic can be defined.
- The topic is not too controversial or complicated.
- It should be possible to collect data on the topic in practice and to improve patient care.
- Preferably there should exist well-developed national or regional guidelines and recommendations.
- The topic should be capable of holding the interest and commitment of the participants.

In order to select such topics a *structured group procedure* is recommended. The first step may be identifying relevant problems and needs in the practices of the participants. Sources of information on specific needs and problems are, for instance (Irvine 1991; Baker and Presley 1990):

- routine statistics (for example, morbidity data, data from insurers);
- formal external evaluations of the practices;
- critical incidents, special events;

- complaints of patients (formal or informal);
- needs, priorities, or uncertainties felt by the participants.

The various possible topics should be exchanged in the peer group in a structured manner. One or several topics are selected and these topics are defined precisely. In many instances this implies that the scope of the topic is also restricted. Methods for the group selection of a topic include brainstorming, the focus method, and the nominal-group method (Donabedian 1980; Fink *et al.* 1984; Mills *et al.* 1988; Ramirez and Shepperd 1988).

Brainstorming

Here the goal is to generate as many ideas as possible. Without debate, participants formulate their needs and possible topics. These are recorded on a flip-chart. When there are no new topics any more, the ideas are ordered systematically in clusters; comparable ideas are combined. A restricted, well-organized list is developed and selection is made using the criteria for topic selection mentioned above.

Focus method

This is also a very open and facilitating method. Ideas are again generated by the participants. In this method, however, participants react to each other continuously, each taking a certain opinion a stage further. All ideas and needs are recorded. After the meeting, one participant studies the ideas, summarizes the information, and makes a proposal of topics that are valued most highly by all the participants. The list is authorized by the group during the next meeting.

Nominal-group method

This method is less interactive. The procedure starts with each participant writing down some topics. In one round in the group all the ideas are presented, recorded on a flip-chart, and clarified, when necessary, without debate. Next, each participants writes down the five most attractive topics and their relevance for general practice care. This activity results in an rank order for the whole group.

Of course, combinations of these methods may be applied in order to select topics. Once a topic has been selected it is important to define it precisely and possibly restrict it to the most important aspects. For example:

- accessibility of the practice: waiting times for routine consultations;
- diabetes care: check-up routines in diabetes type II patients;
- antibiotic prescribing: prescriptions of antibiotics in otitis media in patients under and over two years of age.

SELECTING OR SETTING OF GUIDELINES AND CRITERIA

The importance of guidelines and criteria for peer review was discussed in Chapter 2. Ideally, use is made of guidelines which have been developed on a national or regional scale, have a sound scientific basis, and are broadly accepted in the profession. These external guidelines can then be used for local or practice-based setting of criteria and objectives for practice performance. Guideline development is not easy: it takes considerable time and demands specific skills. Participants in peer review are recommended to use what is available as a basis for the development of their own practice criteria and targets.

In order to translate external guidelines into specific protocols for GP or practice performance the following activities have to be performed:

- the definition of indicators for good quality, based on key elements of a certain topic;
- the definition of criteria for these indicators: precise statements which can be identified as achieved or not achieved;
- finally, a statement can be made on the target for a practice or a care provider: the extent to which the criteria should be achieved.

When guidelines for general practice care are not available on a national or regional scale, which may be the case frequently, a structured procedure is recommended for developing realistic criteria as part of the peer review process. A consensus method for doing this is described in Chapter 8.

Generally speaking, good guidelines for general practice should be (Grol 1993) (Table 7.3):

- *Valid*: they should be based on a sound analysis of the scientific literature and on rigorous exchange of clinical experience.
- *Reliable*: two groups should produce the same guidelines, provided that they had the same information. Also different GPs should apply the guidelines in the same clinical situations consistently.
- *Applicable and relevant*: the guidelines should be formulated from the perspective of the general practice situation. They should focus on the crucial questions that GPs have when they are confronted with patients' problems and fit into the problem-solving activities of day- to-day care. Interviews among GPs disclosed, for instance, that in the case of diabetes care the GPs struggled in particular with weight reduction and dietary adherence in older obese patients. In the case of tonsillitis in a young adult problems were whether it was infectious mononucleosis and whether to prescribe an antibiotic. Guidelines will be helpful when they provide answers to such questions. It is important to assure clinical relevance by testing the consensus guidelines on a small scale and adapting them on the basis of this experience before implementing them fully.
- *Comprehensive and specific*: if guidelines are to be useful for peer review they need to describe clearly the specific situations and patient populations to which they apply, and the exact conditions under which the performance is appropriate or inappropriate. They must also include major relevant factors, such as disease severity or co-morbidity.

Table 7.3 *Criteria for guidelines development in peer review*

Valid	Rigorous analysis of scientific literature
	Adequate use of clinical experience
Reliable	Formalized consensus discussions
	Strict procedures for agreement on guidelines
Relevant and applicable	Guidelines written from general practice perspective
	Guidelines answer questions GPs have
	Application in daily care is easy
Comprehensive	Guidelines identify populations and situations
	They describe conditions under which performance is
	inappropriate
	Inclusive of major relevant factors
Flexible	Guidelines identify exceptions
	Room for clinical judgements, patient preferences, and
	variation with setting
Clear and well organized	Form and language linked to daily practice
	Very specific criteria, objectives
	Presentation in a logical, well-organized form

- *Flexible*: guidelines defined by the group should not be too strict, but offer room for the clinical judgement of the care provider, for patient preferences, and for different practice structures.
- *Clear and understandable*: the guidelines should be written down in a logical, well-organized format and should be formulated in clear and unambiguous language. Precise terminology and the avoidance of abstract terms is important. Presentation in the form of a flow-chart following the care provision process will help care providers in general practice to use it in daily care. Short summaries will also stimulate use.

OBSERVING PRACTICE AND COLLECTING DATA

In order to collect data on actual practice performance feasible instruments are needed. Instruments for collecting data and procedures for performing the collection and analysis of these data are usually available; sometimes they have to be developed by the members of the peer group. Examples and further information on how to develop your own instruments for data collection can be found in the literature on audit (for example Irvine 1991; Smith 1992; Lawrence and Schofield 1993), and many are offered in Part III of this book. Several sources of information can be used (Table 7.4) and several people or organizations can collect the data:

Table 7.4   *Examples of data sources and collection methods in the audit of diabetes type II patients*

Indicators	Criteria	Method of data collection
Structure		
Is the diabetes population of the practice known?	Is the diabetes population marked in the record system?	Observation of record system
Process		
Does surveillance of diabetes patients take place?	Was the blood pressure measured in the past year?	Review chart Patient questionnaire
Is prescription behaviour adequate?	Was first-choice medication used?	Self-monitoring Review chart Date from pharmacist Patient questionnaire
Outcome		
Is the health status of patients acceptable?	Is the glycosylated haemoglobin level acceptable?	Self-recording Chart review Data from laboratory

Source of data?

- patients
- GPs
- practice assistant/nurse
- practice
- hospital
- pharmacy
- funders
- central boards
- etc.

Who collects data?

- GP
- practice staff
- colleagues
- hospital
- trained observers
- funders
- research institutes
- GP organizations
- etc

The actual collection of data on practice performance is generally carried out by the members of the group between meetings. It is very important to make specific arrangements for collecting data, in order to prevent misunderstandings or incompatible information. For example:

- Which aspects of care will be included?
- Which patients will be included, which will not?
- How many patients will be involved (minimum/maximum)?
- How long is the period of data collection?
- Who is responsible for analysis?

EVALUATING THE QUALITY OF CARE

Depending on the specific topic and the method selected for peer review, an analysis of the data takes place during or before the peer review meeting. There are several possibilities, for example:

- One care provider evaluates the performance of one colleague (for example, during practice observation or sitting in the consulting room, or during a peer review meeting).
- One care provider is evaluated by all the peer review group members during a meeting.
- One group member or an external person analyses the data before a meeting to support the evaluation of care during the meeting.
- The data are analysed by means of a computer programme, the results are interpreted and discussed during a meeting.

The analysis may be primarily qualitative in nature, for example when the peer review is focused at communication skills or educating the patient. It may be quantitative, for example when data on self-recording sheets are used to compare performance with guidelines. Or it may be a mixture of the two.

Analysis of data and evaluation of the quality of patient care in a peer review process must be carried out in a structured and rigorous manner. This convinces participants that the peer review is taking place in a careful way and that all important aspects of performance are being fully considered.

FEEDBACK

The presentation of well-based comments and criticism on the performance of a care provider by a colleague or by a group of colleagues is one of the essential elements of improvement by peer review. It is at the heart of the process. For most professionals, comments and feedback by people whom they respect or who are involved in the same kind of work are the most important sources for reflection on and change of their own routines. Giving and receiving feedback during peer review, however, is also one of the most difficult tasks for the members. Some points may be considered in running this part of the process smoothly:

- When the feedback is concerned with very objective data that are compared with very explicit criteria, the message generally is straightforward. However, when the criteria are more subjective and the data are less concrete or more qualitative in nature, it is difficult to be sure whether the feedback is 'true'. Discussions regarding the accuracy and validity of the data should precede discussion concerning their implications.

- Criticism must serve the learning process of the group members. It is not a means for blaming, reassuring, or punishing people nor for taking revenge. It should *help* the auditees to get more awareness of the strong and weak points in their performance.
- Feedback is best concerned with performance data compared with agreed guidelines and criteria. Interpretations and subjective evaluations that are not related to these guidelines are best avoided. There is a tendency to mould criticism into good advice ('You'd do better to take more time for things') or to make a personal evaluation of a colleague ('You are so authoritarian' or 'If you ask me, you're terrified of making mistakes'). Such pieces of advice do not usually serve to help auditees in becoming conscious of the gaps in their performance and should be avoided. Restrict, therefore, feedback to detailed judgements based on the agreed guidelines. Auditees can draw their own conclusions, if necessary, with the help of the group.
- Criticism should be explicit, understandable, and well presented with sufficient evidence and clarification. Observers should be very precise about how they arrived at the judgement. This prevents the giving of general favourable or derogatory assessments.
- The feedback should be positive and stimulating. Auditees must be encouraged to reflect on their performance and to adopt new patterns of behaviour, and must not lose their self-confidence. It is therefore essential to consider also what the auditee does well! This is often neglected, because people feel it speaks for itself and because some people find it difficult to give others positive feedback or to receive it themselves. It is nevertheless an essential part of peer review.
- The peer review members, however, should not treat their colleagues with kid gloves, thereby neglecting to give essential evaluations or enfeebling their force. Experience has shown that peer review can be a disappointment if one is too nice or spares the auditee from criticism.

Giving and receiving feedback

- Feedback serves the learning process of the group members.
- Feedback is preferably concerned with performance data compared with agreed guidelines and criteria, not with personal interpretations or moral judgements.
- Feedback is explicit, understandable, and well organized; it is presented with sufficient supporting evidence.
- Feedback is positive and stimulating; however, beware of sparing a colleague.
- Feedback is directed at routines, at set patterns in the performance, not at individual cases.
- In receiving feedback the auditee bewares of becoming defensive.

- Criticism is preferably not focused on individual contacts between care providers and patients, but on the general pattern in the performance, as shown in a great number of cases or contacts. Otherwise one is inclined to weaken the feedback because of extraordinary circumstances in a particular case. There are usually valid reasons for performance in each contact with a patient. Peer review, however, is about improving fixed routines and patterns of working.
- During the presentation of feedback it helps for the auditee to speak first, identifying the good aspects and then the deficiencies in his or her performance. Thereafter the auditee who is receiving the feedback listens carefully and makes notes of what is said, without debate! Ask for clarifications, but don't defend yourself and don't argue about whether the feedback is fair or true. Afterwards the feedback can be used by the auditee to select objectives for change in individual or practice performance.

This giving feedback to each other forms the link between the identification of performance and implementation of change in general practice care.

PLANNING AND IMPLEMENTING CHANGES

Feedback received from your peers can offer a very powerful stimulus in bringing about desirable changes in practice performance, provided that sufficient attention is given to planning of such changes during the peer review process. Frequently, group members feel that the review process is complete after they have given and received comments on their work and that of colleagues. The step towards drawing consequences from the feedback is often neglected or undertaken very hesitantly. However, it is clear from many studies that feedback is a necessary but not sufficient step towards actual changes in performance.

Therefore, this next step of planning and implementing changes should also be carried out in a rigorous and structured way. It consists of the following activities (see Fig. 7.1):

1. Identifying areas for changing and setting specific goals that can be achieved in a relatively short time. Each participant or practice selects the specific goals for change that are most relevant for their own working situation, with the help of colleagues. The peer group takes particular care that individual members of the peer group or colleagues do not set their objectives too high. One or two achievable goals or a plan for changing step by step is preferred.
2. Identifying and discussing specific barriers for achieving the desired changes. These barriers may be diverse and related to personal aspects of the care providers (knowledge, attitudes, skills) or to the social network, the premises of the practice, or structural factors (see example in Table 7.5). Sometimes data on these problems have to be gathered in a systematic way, for example by means of a survey or by methods offered by the 'total quality management' approaches from industry (such as flow-charts, cause–effect diagrams or Pareto analysis (Berwick *et al.* 1990; Ellis and Whittington 1993). Often,

Table 7.5   *Opinions of GPs on problems in following guidelines for the manage-ment of diabetes mellitus II (survey among 453 GPs)*

	This is a problem (%)
A proactive approach is necessary	63
Every patient is different	58
Specialists take care of many of the diabetes patients	45
There is no financial reward for changing	38
It costs extra time and work	33
I have doubts as to the relevance of the guidelines	24

however, a brainstorming in the peer group will illuminate most barriers sufficiently.

In discussion, individuals or practices may identify different barriers. But frequently members of a peer group prove to have many problems in achieving change in common. Becoming aware of comparable problems in achieving desired alterations may give relief and support to participants.

3. Planning the implementation of change. The members of the group help each other in finding solutions for the problems identified. In this way strategy can be developed with specific actions directed to the identified barriers and problems. When there are problems relevant to the majority of the peer group a joint strategy for the whole group may be selected.

4. Carrying out the plan for change. This may be done partly inside the group, partly outside it. The support of colleagues may be particularly useful in demonstrating alternative behaviour, in giving explicit solutions for specific problems, in making arrangements for helping each other, and in agreeing on a formal contract for implementing the changes. Between sessions the participants have to experiment actively with the agreed new routines or practice.

Quality assurance finds its value in bringing about improvements in actual patient care. Therefore, as much time and attention in the peer review process should be devoted to stimulating and implementing changes as to developing guidelines or collecting and discussing data.

FOLLOW-UP

The final step in the peer review process, the one that closes the cycle, is that of evaluating whether the participants succeeded and whether they achieved their preset goals for improving practice performance. This implies the following actions:

- Repeat measurements: rehearsal of the data collection and analysis.
- When the targets are not achieved, the causes of the failure are analysed. Was it due to:

- – unrealistic objectives or criteria; do these have to be adapted?
- – efforts of the participants: did they really do their utmost to bring about the agreed changes?
- – factors concerning social circumstances or the structure of the practice?
- A plan is made for further actions: the criteria and targets may be adapted, or a new, more effective plan may be made for bringing about change in the practice.

CONCLUSIONS

Peer review is a cyclic, structured process in which time and attention are distributed between the important steps in the process:

- preparing the ground;
- selecting a topic;
- defining explicit criteria or objectives;
- data collection;
- evaluation of current performance;
- planning and implementing changes;
- follow-up

In the following chapters some methods for use in peer review or audit among colleagues are presented. The methods differ regarding their focus: some give more emphasis to selecting a relevant problem to solve, others focus more on evaluating and changing care (Table 7.6). Varying the methods used makes peer review more interesting as well as more effective for learning and improving.

Table 7.6 *Methods for peer review and their focus*

Method	Selecting relevant problems	Selecting or setting criteria	Observing practice and evaluating care	Planning and implementing change
Consensus development in peer review groups	*	*		
Use of data on clinical performance		*	*	*
Use of audio- or videotaped consultations			*	*
Mutual practice observation				*
Practice-based quality circles	*			*
Case and critical incident analysis	*			*

8 Developing guidelines and criteria in peer review

In Chapter 2 of this book we highlighted the importance in peer review of having explicit criteria based on recognized guidelines. In this chapter three methods for developing such criteria and guidelines in a peer group are presented (see box on pp. 63–4)

- developing criteria for peer review or quality improvement on the basis of available guidelines and protocols;
- developing guidelines and criteria on the basis of literature analysis and consensus discussion;
- developing guidelines and criteria by means of reflection on current experiences and routines in the practice.

Being involved in developing guidelines for high quality in patient care using consensus discussions can be a very valuable, educational experience (see example, North of England Study of Standards and Performance 1992). When it is carried out on a local or practice level, it may help care providers to develop a sense of 'ownership' of the guidelines. Developing guidelines should take place in a rigorous way, through a standardized procedure, in order to prevent obsolete performance being selected as an objective so reinforcing the *status quo*, or dominant group members with outspoken convictions forcing their ideas on a peer group. This demands specific interpersonal and technical skills and skills with regard to analysing the available literature.

DEVELOPING CRITERIA ON THE BASIS OF AVAILABLE GUIDELINES AND PROTOCOLS

In order to speed up the process of peer review, it is advisable to start with available guidelines, developed by other groups or organizations (for example, the guidelines in the instruments offered in Part III of this book). These can be used to agree criteria and targets that the group members or a practice team wish to achieve.

After a specific topic has been selected, the available guidelines have been spread among the members as homework, and the participants have studied the recommendations carefully, the session can start. It is handled in the following manner.

Defining the topic

A discussion takes place on which aspects of the topic are seen by the participants as most relevant or most problematic. This leads to a delineation of the topic and a selection of the guidelines that will be used.

Consensus development in the North of England Study of Standards and Performance in General Practice (1992)

In the north of England local small groups of general practitioner trainers, sometimes supported by a medical specialist, have developed standards, by means of a structured procedure, for a series of general practice topics. The procedure included reading literature, examining existing standards, developing branching logic skills, and group discussions. Each group developed its own standards and the results were shared with the other groups. In this way, expertise was exchanged among a large group of GPs in the region. The impact of setting standards on practice was evaluated. Some improvements were found in the prescription and follow-up behaviour of GPs and in the patients' compliance with medication and in their health. Evaluation of the developmental process revealed that standard setting is not easy and calls for interpersonal, technical, and clinical skills.

Discussing the guidelines

The recommendations in the 'external' guidelines are critically discussed by the group members. Is there support for these guidelines in the group? Which recommendations are not shared? Are there proposals for adaption of the guidelines? This stage should be taken rather quickly. The discussion has to be to the point. When members of the group disagree on certain guidelines, arguments for and against are collected and discussed briefly. If necessary more information may need to be researched until an agreement is reached.

Developing guidelines and criteria in peer review

Developing criteria on the basis of available guidelines and protocols
- defining the topic;
- discussing the guidelines;
- translating guidelines into specific criteria/targets;
- implementing the guidelines.

Developing guidelines on the basis of the literature and consensus discussions
- exploration of the topic;
- dividing tasks;
- discussing the draft;
- testing the guidelines;
- final version, arrangements.

Developing guidelines by means of reflection on current routines
- recording performance;
- comparing recordings;
- making underlying values explicit;
- deciding the guidelines;
- formulating arrangements.

Translating the guidelines into specific criteria and targets

The recommendations are transformed into feasible objectives for practice performance, agreed by the participants, for example:

- the maximum waiting time for a patient before a consultation should be 15 minutes;
- diabetes type II patients should have a fasting blood glucose value under 8 mmol/l. This criterion should be satisfied for 90 per cent of patients.

Individual members make proposals which then are discussed and adapted by the other participants. Particular attention is given to making the objectives very clear, specific, and unambiguous.

Implementing the guidelines

Arrangements are made for the use of the guidelines in practice, for evaluating care with them, and for further discussions on their feasibility.

DEVELOPING GUIDELINES ON THE BASIS OF THE LITERATURE AND CONSENSUS DISCUSSIONS

When there are no satisfactory external guidelines available for a selected topic, which may be the case frequently, the group may develop their own. They can proceed in the following fashion.

Exploration of the topic

Participants introduce cases from practice, concerning the selected topic. They describe how they are confronted with the problem and what their current routines are. This is helpful as an orientation and for warming up. Questions to be answered at this stage are:

- What exactly are the problems with regard to this topic?
- Which aspects of the topics are most problematic and need guidance?
- What do we know about actual performance?

The most important problems and questions in day-to-day care will become clear in this discussion, so defining the areas that the guidelines will have to cover will be the result of this step.

Dividing tasks

One or two of the group members are selected to analyse the literature, consult experts, study guidelines or protocols from other sources, and prepare a draft. These participants will bring concrete proposals to the next meeting. The draft guidelines are preferably written down in an orderly, well-organized fashion, for example as a flow-chart, a decision tree, or a summary.

Discussing the draft

A structured discussion takes place, in which the guidelines are rigorously screened and evaluated. For each stage in the guidelines:

- arguments pro are identified;
- arguments contra are identified;
- a brief discussion is held to see whether new arguments come to the fore;
- a decision is taken.

Then the next stage is discussed. The participants, who prepared the draft, write down the comments and the decisions and revise the guidelines afterwards. The discussion of the draft may have raised questions that require new literature analysis or consultation of specific experts.

Testing the guidelines

An arrangement may be made to test the guidelines on a small scale in practice to see if they are feasible in daily care. The experiences are used during the next meeting to adjust the draft guidelines.

Final version, arrangements

During the next session a new proposal, based on the new information, will be available and discussed, preferably in a brief manner. When consensus is reached arrangements in the peer review group are made about how to apply the guidelines. Arrangements can be made to implement them: a plan for changing practice. The guidelines can be translated into specific criteria as was described before, and used as a basis for data collection.

DEVELOPING GUIDELINES BY MEANS OF REFLECTION ON CURRENT ROUTINES

Another approach, when feasible guidelines or protocols are lacking, is developing guidelines based on existing routines. Differences in the routines and underlying values of the peer group members are the basis for discussion in achieving consensus guidelines. The method for doing this properly is described extensively by van de Rijdt *et al.* (1988). The following steps are taken in the peer review process after having selected, defined, and marked off a suitable topic.

Recording performance

The participants record their performance during a number of contacts with real patients on a standard record sheet (Fig. 8.1). Clear instructions are given to the group before the recording begins. For example:

- whether age limits are to be imposed;
- whether only the first contact with a patient is to be recorded or the following ones also;
- whether specific conditions or inclusion criteria are to be applied;
- how many patients have to be recorded.

A record sheet is filled in, immediately or as soon as possible after the contact with a patient. At least three to four record sheets per participant should be filled in. The record sheets are brought to the peer group meeting. Participants prepare for this meeting by studying their own sheets and considering their existing routines and their opinions on adequate performance.

● **Patient's name:**	**Age:**	**Male/female**

Exceptional factors, relevant details from the patient's case history:

- Patient's reasons for coming to the doctor:

- Which points from the history did you pursue in depth:

- Information derived from this questioning:

Provisional description of the problem:

- Did you carry out any physical examination:

- Information derived from this:

- Did you carry out additional examinations:

- Information derived from these:

Definition of the problem:

- What was your policy (treatment, advice, referral, etc.):

Fig. 8.1   Record sheet for peer review (van de Rijdt *et al.* 1988).

Comparing recordings

Several record sheets are read out loud by one member. The performance patterns thus revealed are then commented on by the other members of the group. Participants react on:

- what strikes them about the cases;
- what they approve of;
- what they do differently themselves.

Review group members learn from each other in this way, considering similarities and differences in performance.

It is impossible to discuss each case of each participant in detail. It is, however, important that all members have the opportunity to bring in cases and get some comments on their routines.

Making underlying values and principles explicit

The previous stage will have revealed the extent of correspondences and differences to be found between the participants' policies. This stage is directed to consideration of the underlying reasons and values: 'Why do I work as I do?' The participants 'cross-question' each other on the basis for specific routines. This confrontation will raise many questions, which require further analysis of the literature or consultation of experts. This will become homework for one or more participants, who will report back to the group on their findings during the next meeting of the group.

Deciding the guidelines

A structured discussion takes place in which guidelines are developed. Members who studied the literature or consulted the experts bring in their findings. Element after element is discussed:

- arguments pro are identified;
- arguments contra are identified;
- compromises are proposed;
- decisions are taken.

The final conclusions are written down very precisely.

Formulating arrangements

During this stage the participants indicate what they intend to adjust or change in their own performance in view of the guidelines which have been developed in previous stages. A plan for implementing guidelines is made, as well as arrangements for recording performance in the practice.

9 Peer review by means of audio or video recordings

Peer review employing audio or video recordings of patient encounters has acquired a considerable tradition and has shown its value in a variety of situations. Large studies on general practice performance were carried out on the basis of such material (for example, Verby *et al.* 1979; Grol *et al.* 1988b; Smith *et al.* 1991). Exceptionally good experiences have been acquired with audiotapes in peer review and in the instruction of GP trainees (Grol *et al.* 1988a). In Great Britain a tradition of audit with videotapes has been developed (for example, Pendleton *et al.* 1984). Both methods offer a very good basis for the audit of consultation skills in a group of care providers in general practice (5–10 participants). The audit is livened up due to the fact that the participants are directly confronted with a real consultation situation. Initially, it may prove threatening: having recording apparatus in the consulting room takes some getting used to, as does asking the patient's permission to record and having one's personal performance evaluated in the peer review group. In our experience, the difficulties soon fade, and the use of video- or audiotapes gradually becomes a greatly prized aid in the quality improvement process.

AUDIO AND VIDEO RECORDINGS

The submission of patient consultations on audio- or videotape should be well prepared by auditees. The success of the meeting depends to a large extent on the material brought it by auditees and on the manner in which they have prepared themselves.

Audio recording

- Instal the cassette recorder in the surgery in such a way that it is outside the visual field of the patient.
- Use a separate, sensitive microphone that preferably covers both the consultation and the examination rooms. Test the location of the microphone properly beforehand.
- It is also possible to use a portable recorder with a separate microphone that is carried by the care provider.
- During an arbitrary surgery hour, record a tape of 90 minutes. Make a note of the patients visiting the surgery and their complaints.
- For each patient, after the consultation, fill in the form 'Registration form for consultation skills' (Fig. 9.1) in as detailed a way as possible.

GP:	Date:	Counter start: End:
Patient: Age: Gender: m/f		
Complaint, reason for encounter:		
Physical examinations performed:		
Laboratory tests:		
Diagnosis/working hypothesis:		
Prescribed medication:	Referral to: Date follow-up appointment:	

Fig. 9.1   Registration form for consultation skills.

- When the surgery hour is over or when the tape is full, the auditee should play the tape and select a number of consultations or parts of consultations for the audit group. In general choose encounters that are neither too difficult nor too simple. Do not select protracted consultations, consultations involving complex psychosocial issues, or consultations that are poorly audible.
- Note the recorder counter readings of the selected pieces. Put the tape at the beginning of the first piece to be presented, in order to save time during the meeting.

Video recording

When using a video recorder some extra factors are relevant:

- Use a video recording system that is compatible with the system of the apparatus used for playing the tape in the group (usually VHS).
- Use a wide-angle lens so that most of the consultation room is on the screen. Position the camera in such a way that the faces of both the doctor and the patient are visible. If that is impossible, concentrate on the face of the patient. Preferably install an extended, separate microphone on the desk. The internal microphone of the camera is often inadequate.
- Use a system that permits a recording of three to four hours, so that an entire surgery hour can be recorded. Switching off the tape during the surgery hour is both difficult to remember and disturbing.
- It is handy to have a remote control with which the camera can be paused or switched off.

- Modern video cameras have a good exposure regulation. Extra lighting is usually unnecessary.

For more details see Pendleton *et al.* (1984).

CONSENT OF THE PATIENT

For both audio and video recordings, informed consent in writing of the patient is mandatory. The request should be made in such a way that the patient feels perfectly free to refuse. The doctor must also ask for permission to discuss the recording with other doctors. Furthermore, patients should be able to go back on their consent. All of this demands a clear explanation concerning the purpose of the recording, without inducing unnecessary anxiety, for example: 'I would like to record our talk on audio/videotape for my own continuing education. The tape will be played in a group of general practitioners, who will then comment on my way of working. Are you agreeable to that?' Experience shows that patients rarely have objections. When they do, or when they hesitate, do not insist.

THE PEER REVIEW SESSION

For peer review there is a fixed procedure and a number of clear steps that are followed precisely each time. In that way the participants quickly become familiar with the procedure. The duration of the meeting depends on the number of consultations that are reviewed. The procedure is explained step by step below. An overview is presented in the box.

Steps in peer review using audio or video recordings

A. Preparation
- Review of the previous meeting.
- The individual objectives of group members are agreed.
- The criteria to be used in the peer review are agreed.
- Possibly: splitting up a large group into subgroups (four to five persons).
- The GP about to be audited introduces the consultation material.
- The tasks in the evaluation are divided up.

B. Collecting and evaluating data on performance
- The group listens to the tape, takes notes on or makes summaries of the care provision process.

- Group members analyse the data, comparing performance to criteria.
- Summary of the findings: observers each select some strong and weak points in the performance.

C.   Feedback
- The auditee gives a short personal response first.
- One observer presents a selection of strong and weak points.
- Other group members add information.
- The auditee makes notes; may ask for clarification but does not interject with comments.

D.   Planning and implementing change.
- After the presentation of feedback the auditee responds to the criticism in a general manner first.
- Afterwards the auditee gives a review of some important aspects of performance that require change; specific points are selected.
- A plan for change is developed with help of the group.
- The auditee writes a short report on the plan for change.
- During the next meeting the progress is discussed.

A.   Preparation

At the start of each session one might spend a little time in reviewing the previous session and the effect it has had on the participants since:

- What have the group members done in between the sessions with the new skills and attitudes which they developed at the previous meeting?
- How did they feel the meeting had gone? Are any improvements in the management of the meeting required?

A moment of reflection like this can serve as a warming up, but should not drag on too long.

A decision has to be made next on the aspects of the consultation which will be considered during the peer review process. The use of audio or video recordings is particularly useful for reviewing general consultation skills, such as structuring the care provision process, communicating with patients, taking a history, and giving information and instruction. Instruments for reviewing these important aspects of general practice performance are presented in Part III of this book. Groups are recommended to select one particular aspect of performance to use in a peer review, for example patient education or the doctor–patient relationship. However, instruments developed by others may also be used (for example, Pendleton *et al.* 1984).

When the group is large (more than eight persons), it is advisable to split up in subgroups (four to five persons). Peer review using audio or video recordings works particularly well in the safe setting of a small, intimate group.

Next the general practitioner who is about to be audited says a few words about the material he or she is going to present to the group:

- Who the tapes are about: the sex and age of patients, whether the contacts are new or old, some background, and the type of complaints. The introduction to the contacts can be sketchy. Explaining exactly what is the matter with the patient and details of the past history can be left out or, if at all relevant, is best discussed afterwards.
- The particular reason for choosing these contacts: any special questions to be put to the group members about these contacts, or any particular aspect to which they should pay special attention.

If the audit is to run smoothly it is important to supervise the number of contacts that are presented, their nature, and their length.

- The number of contacts: When reviewing, it is not so much a question of how GPs work in individual cases, as what in their practice routines meets the criteria for good general practice performance and what does not. It is necessary to listen to a number of contacts in order to be able to make a judgement, and in doing so an eye must be kept on the clock. From experience, it would seem that two to three contacts or parts of contacts, totalling a maximum of 20 minutes, offer a reasonable basis for an evaluation of performance. An alternative is to involve as many GPs as possible in the review during a session. In this case, each participant is restricted to one consultation or even a part of it. Members will also improve by observing their colleagues.
- Type of contact: Some participants tend to choose to introduce exceptional cases or cases which they found very difficult. But as has already been pointed out, it is the usual performance elements, present in all contacts, that are important in review. Preferably one should choose middle-of-the-road general practice contacts, especially in the beginning, from which the person being audited can learn something: not too difficult and not too easy, and, particularly, not too long.
- Length of the contact: The capability of the audit group to listen spellbound to consultation material is limited. One must not forget that there has to be a good deal of time for the assessment round and for attempting to formulate improvements. Taking all this into consideration, 20 minutes of listening is the maximum. If necessary, one can stop a tape during a specific contact.

Finally, evaluation tasks are divided, when necessary. It may be practical to give the various members different tasks. Some will be listening and giving attention to specific aspects of the performance, while others are focused on other elements of the provided care. For example, when the group has chosen to use the guidelines for general consultation skills, one part of the group may focus on structuring the consultation, while another may be involved in evaluating the doctor–patient relationship.

B.   Collecting and evaluating data on performance

The tape is started and the participants look at or listen to the presented consultations. Whilst the tape is being run, the best thing to do is to make a short resumé of the contacts. One notes down certain of the GP's sentences literally, especially at the explanatory phase, during the explanation stage, and in the stage of formulating a plan. Physical examination can be recorded by key words. This is also a suitable method for recording the patient's reactions. Whilst listening, it is better not to make judgements and criticisms about specific skills. It is far better to do it afterwards, using the collected data (the notes) as a guide and following the criteria, otherwise there is a danger of pursuing very subjective impressions.

During or immediately after listening to the tape the auditee presents additional data on performance from the recording sheet (Fig. 9.1) that are not assessable from the tape. This is especially necessary when audiotape is being used.

Once the tape is turned off, time must be taken for group members to analyse the notes which they have collected and compare the performance with the agreed criteria. First the different consultations are evaluated separately. Next the findings of several consultations are summarized to gain an overall impression:

- What are the strong points in the working style of this GP?
- What are the shortcomings, the gaps?

The evaluator selects one or two most representative strong and one or two weak points, to discuss in the feedback stage, and prepares a clear, understandable, and constructive presentation of the feedback.

It is important to restrict the number of critical comments. When a group of colleagues presents a long list of remarks, it is difficult for the auditee to remember or to handle these. When the most important shortcomings are discussed, the chance is bigger that the auditee really uses the comments in improving performance.

C. Feedback

Before the group members begin commenting, auditees must be given the chance to give their reactions to their performance if they are so inclined. A moment like that also enables auditees to let off steam. There is a danger that the tension level has risen, whilst viewing or listening to the tapes. By working off some of this tension auditees will be more open to receiving criticism. The idea is not that auditees themselves start to give a formal review of their stronger and weaker points. The response should be short, and, for example, reflect how it feels when listening to one's own performance or receiving criticism.

There is an inclination to react to or to discuss comments immediately. This may cause a more tense atmosphere. It is better if auditees do not react during the presentation of the feedback nor account for their performance. They should let the criticism make its impact, write down as much as possible of what is said. If certain critical comments are unclear, they may want to ask for further explanations.

The evaluation round itself may be organized in the following fashion. This may seem rather rigid, but at the beginning of the peer review process it is advisable to allow the feedback to be rather artificial and schoolish. One group member gives feedback: a maximum of two strong and two weak points, with arguments for these evaluations based on the use of the agreed criteria. When other group members have been concentrating on the same skills, they present additional comments. Next, other group members may give comments on other skills.

In the evaluation rounds auditees are the focus of attention. They may make a selection from the criticism offered, even if the members of the group are not in agreement on all aspects.

At a later stage one may be more flexible during the evaluation rounds. The criticism can be more geared to the auditees' requests. Other criteria, instruments, and methods of peer review may be added. For example, when auditees have been observed in the consulting room by a colleague (see Chapter 11) the results of this evaluation can be used to complement the audio- or videotape analysis. This may enhance the assessment of performance considerably.

D.   Planning and implementing changes

Auditees have, during the evaluation round, noted as much as possible of what has been discussed. Once the round has finished they are invited to respond to the criticism in a general fashion, for example by using questions like:

- What part of the criticism can you go along with?
- What do you find difficult to accept?
- What is unclear?

Auditees may go through the points of criticism again, ask questions, or give extra information about the reasons for acting in a certain way. This activity may help them to absorb the comments. Besides, it is nice when the participants notice that the auditee has incorporated their remarks. It is important that the auditee also discusses the positive comments.

Next, auditees are stimulated to delve deeper into the criticism and to select aspects of their performance that require change:

- Which points are most important to you?
- What do you have to pay special attention to in the near future?
- Select one or two important aspects, that you will work on in the next month.

Since it is very difficult to implement more than a few changes in routines at a time, auditees should restrict themselves in their intentions.

In this way a specific plan for change is made. The auditee may be inclined, once the remarks have been made quite clear, to respond with 'Well, now I know, don't I.' Little enthusiasm is shown for organizing ways of effecting a change in behaviour. This may arise because some time is needed for the criticism to sink in or for the acceptance that things could really be done differently. One might be able to help an auditee to make the step forward at moments like this with questions like:

- Have you any idea as to how you can change these routines?
- What is exactly the problem you are experiencing with changing your performance?
- What in particular do you need to enable you to do things differently?

- Do you need more knowledge or skills or do you need to change structural or organizational aspects of the practice performance?

The barriers to achieving the desired change are explored thoroughly first by auditees themselves. Only after that can group members be asked to give suggestions or propose alternatives.

When time is available new routines may be practised by role playing. One of the group members is the patient. One of the contacts on the audio- or videotape is played. The auditee is asked to experiment with the proposed alternative performance. The group members comment on this performance afterwards and make suggestions as to how the desired improvements could be achieved. Possibly, the role play can be repeated.

In some instances it becomes clear that the shortcomings in performance, in particular in communication with the patient, have to do with personal features, values, needs, experiences, or uncertainties of the auditee. Changing these may require considerable efforts and is *not* part of a peer review process. The GP should be referred to other methods such as a counselling group, a Balint group, or a personal training group.

It is important for auditees to make a short report of the important training points after their performance has been judged and after a plan for change has been made. It forces the auditee think once again about the strong points and the gaps in performance. Moreover when the points appear in black and white, they gain in stature and become a stronger stimulus actually to carry out the changes. At the same time they offer the opportunity at a later date of seeing what the intentions for change were and whether the auditee has succeeded in achieving change.

At the beginning of the next meeting one may stop to consider briefly what the auditee has done about implementing the changes in the period between sessions.

10 Use of data on clinical performance in peer review

INTRODUCTION

All general practitioners have developed fixed routines of clinical performance in the course of running their practices. This may mean routinely carrying out certain physical examinations, ordering a certain laboratory test, or prescribing a particular medication for a condition. These routines will be rational in part and based on the most recent scientific information from the literature. In part they may be irrational or represent outdated behaviour or lack of understanding. It is virtually impossible for a practising GP to keep up to date continuously with all the new developments in the field.

For these reasons it is particularly important for GPs to reflect regularly on their clinical routines with colleagues and to discover which of their routines are still adequate and which are questionable. Exchanging data on clinical performance in a peer review process is a particularly valuable and effective method for improving clinical competence and performance.

The approach may consist of exchanging current routine topics like the frequency of performing tests, prescribing medications, or referring to specialists (results of a 'practice activity analysis', see Crombie and Fleming 1988). Insight into the variation in performance may offer a powerful stimulus for studying the rationality of the different routines in more detail. This method has been successfully applied in various countries (UK, Denmark, Netherlands, Portugal).

A disadvantage of this approach is that GPs who perform better than average are not stimulated to change their performance. Also, it is not always clear which performance is desirable. For these reasons it is recommended to use generally accepted guidelines or criteria for peer review on clinical performance (for example, the guidelines developed by working parties or colleges in various countries or the national standards developed by the Dutch College of GPs; more and more of such guidelines will become available in the years to come).

As a help in the peer review process this book presents some practical instruments for data collection and reviewing clinical performance (Chapter 16). The criteria in these instruments may be used or they may be adapted in order to fit better with personal or group preference. They represent generally agreed good general practice care; however, they should not be taken as a 'truth'. Hard evidence for most of the selected criteria in these instruments is not available. They should be seen as a tool in the peer review process, an aid in improving the clinical performance of family doctors.

Some methods of doing this are described below. A series of steps has to be taken and good preparation should precede the peer review.

PREPARATION

The process starts with *selecting a suitable topic* for peer review. Methods for selecting the topic were presented in Chapters 7 and 8. Again, for groups beginning to run peer review it is preferable to chose a topic for which well-developed guidelines and methods for collecting data and evaluating care are already available.

After having agreed on several possible topics, one topic is *explored* in more detail. The participants discuss some representative cases from the practice briefly. This makes clear how care providers in general practice confront this topic in day-to-day care. It clarifies the most important questions and problems with regard to the topic and the crucial decisions that have to be taken. For example a survey among GPs in The Netherlands showed that two major problems that GPs face in managing older patients with type II diabetes are how to get the patients to reduce weight, and when to start medication. By discussing cases in this way, the central aspects of the topic become clear and the focus for peer review is clarified. The topic is *defined precisely* and is restricted to the most relevant aspects (for example, the therapy in acute otitis media, the surveillance of diabetes mellitus type II patients, the physical examination in the case of a patient with shoulder complaints).

SELECTING OR AGREEING ON GUIDELINES AND CRITERIA

Next the group must *select or agree on guidelines and criteria* that will be used in the process. In Chapter 7 it was recommended that the group take some generally accepted guidelines and translate them into criteria or target standards for their own work setting. This in turn guides the data collection required in practice. It may help to use or adapt one of the instruments for clinical performance from this book (Chapter 16), or to follow the procedures described in Chapter 8.

DATA COLLECTION

Arrangements are then made for the actual *collection* of data:

- Which instrument for data collection will be used?
- How many patients will be involved (minimum, maximum)?
- How long will be the period of data collection?
- Who will be responsible for collecting and analysing the data and giving feedback?

Very clear arrangements will contribute to successful peer review. Indeed the process may be considerably damaged if care providers do not understand or do not follow the arrangements so that their data are not comparable.

In Chapter 16 a series of checklists for data collection on the management of common conditions in general practice is presented. The checklists form both a guideline on the basis of which a management protocol can be written, and also a checklist which can be filled out by the GP, preferably immediately after a contact with a patient. They may also be filled out by an observer during or after a patient contact (see Chapter 11).

In order to make a reasonable comparison between the routines of different GPs it is recommended that data are collected for at least five patients (preferably 10 or more), with a selected complaint or condition. There will naturally be differences between each contact depending on the patient's precise problem, but the routine part of the management of the complaint or condition will come out clearly.

EVALUATING DATA ON PERFORMANCE

There are two main methods of evaluating the data: either each GP can aggregate their own results and bring them for discussion, or one member can collect all the data sheets and present the results to the group.

Analysis by the group members themselves

- GPs continue recording until they have 5, 10, or more registration sheets or checklists. They then record on a separate sheet or checklist how many times an action was performed. Any additional actions are added as freehand comments.
- GPs then brings their personal 'aggregated' data to the peer review session. The group splits up into small groups (two to three persons); the participants study each other's data sheets and discuss each other's performance:
  - deviations from the selected criteria;
  - arguments for the deviation.

Analysis and feedback by one of the group members

- The participants send their checklists or registration sheets to one of the members of the group at least one week before the group session.
- This group member analyses the data and designs an overview. The overall results for the group are presented, usually with the participants being anonymous, and the code for each person's individual results being revealed only to that person. Graphics can help in making the presentation striking. Important deviations from the agreed criteria are highlighted.
- Feedback is presented during the group session. Group members each study their own sources and note down gaps in their own practice routine.

Next each member describes important variations affecting their practice. The group selects some of the major deviations from the agreed criteria and discusses them for about 30 minutes:

- Are the agreed criteria or guidelines or criteria feasible?
- Should they be adapted?
- If not, why were they not followed?

Steps in peer review using data on clinical performance

Preparation
- selection of a relevant, suitable topic;
- exploring the topic in more detail;
- focusing on crucial aspects;
- selecting or agreeing on guidelines and criteria;
- developing an instrument for collecting data;
- arrangements on data collection and analysis.

Data collection and evaluation of care
- arrangements for self-recording in the practice;
- collecting data on 5–10 patients;
- analysis of data:
    - by GP: each group member brings aggregated data to session,
    - by one group member: makes an overview of individual and group scores;
- discussing performance and feedback;
- discussing the criteria.

Planning and implementing changes
- each participant selects two or three attainable goals for change
- a plan for implementing these changes is developed;
- the intentions are noted down in the report;
- arrangements for evaluating progress are made.

PLANNING AND IMPLEMENTING CHANGE

After a general discussion on the reasons for deviating from the guidelines, the peer review activities are directed to improving individual clinical performance. It is crucial to reserve sufficient time for this part of the peer review process!

Each participant selects a maximum of two or three specific goals for *changing practice performance*. These goals should be:

- very specific;
- attainable before the next group meeting.

Since it is very difficult to implement more than a few changes in routines at a time, participants should be careful to limit their intentions.

Next, a specific *plan for implementing these changes* is designed. Members in turn introduce their goals for change. These are considered briefly by the group, addressing the following questions:

- How are you going to change these routines?
- Which problems do you expect in achieving these changes?
- What do you need to achieve them: more knowledge/skills and/or structural or organizational changes in your practice?

The barriers to achieving the desired changes and ways of overcoming these barriers are explored thoroughly by the members in turn. Only after the affected members have done this for themselves may colleagues from the group give suggestions or propose alternatives. If necessary, more data are gathered on the specific barriers first.

If a new skill is required and time is available it may be practised in the group, so taking advantage of sharing skills (for example, bandaging, using a glucometer).

CLOSING THE SESSION

It is very important to make a *short report* of the session containing the intended changes of each individual group member. When they have been noted down in black and white, visible for all to see, they gain in stature and imply a stronger obligation for the member actually to carry out the changes.

Finally, *arrangements* for evaluating progress with regard to the intended changes are made. At the start of the next session participants report back briefly on whether they succeeded with the new routines. Later on the data collection and evaluation of the actual performance have to be repeated to see whether the participants did indeed incorporate the changes in their performance. New goals for further improving clinical performance may then be agreed.

11   Mutual practice observation

INTRODUCTION

In this chapter we present methods for observing each other's practices and reviewing each other's consultation skills. These have proven to be very valuable additions to peer review group work and can be easily included as one of the peer review activities.

Mutual practice observation is concerned with one or more care providers observing another care provider at work. This can include inspection of practice premises or observation of practice management. Observers may also be present during contacts with patients, at the surgery, or on home visits. They may even be present during other activities, such as primary care team meetings, administrative work or education meetings. They may collect information in various ways: by direct observation, by questionnaires, by chart audit, or by patient surveys.

The procedure will depend on the aims. The aims may differ for the observer and the observed care provider. The observed person wants to be audited in a systematic and detailed fashion and receive feedback on performance in order to be able to make changes. For observers, the practice observation is, in the first place, an exercise in observing and accurately evaluating a colleague's or another practice's performance. This is followed by exercising their capabilities in giving differentiated and balanced feedback. Furthermore, a process of self-audit takes place: observers may compare the performance of the practice being observed with their own individual or practice performance, and try to find out where the differences are and what that means in terms of their own working methods.

There are a number of advantages and disadvantages of observing one another in practice. Drawbacks are that the visitor may have the same blind spots as the host and that observers only see flashes of what in fact is a continuous process of care. In order to cope with these drawbacks it is necessary to have clear and feasible methods and instruments for evaluating the practice. Feasible methods for practice visiting are increasingly available in countries like the UK (What sort of doctor, Fellowship by assessment, and practice visiting methods to review audit developed by various MAAGs), New Zealand (family medicine training programme) and The Netherlands (evaluation of practice management). The instruments in Part III of this book may be helpful in planning a successful and educational practice visit.

The chief advantage of practice observation by peers lies in the fact that these methods are optimally suited to breaking the relative isolation in which certain general practitioners and practices work. Selective criticism about strong and weak points in the practice routines is given by colleagues in the same profession. At the same time the observers get all kinds of new ideas for running their own practices and for finding solutions to existing problems there. It is also important that the observers experience that they in their own practices are not the only ones struggling with certain problems. Practitioners who have experienced mutual practice visits have been, on the whole, very positive about this type of peer review. It was seen as extremely valuable and instructive for both the observer and the host.

THE PRACTICE OBSERVATION METHODOLOGY

The way in which a practice visit takes place depends on the aims and the arrangements of the various involved persons:

- Two colleagues can arrange a mutual visit, for example as part of a vocational training scheme.
- A group representing a practice team, for example doctor, practice manager, practice nurse, and health visitor, may be received by a similar group in another practice.
- A peer group of care providers from different practices may arrange mutual practice observations as well as discussion of the outcomes of the observation in the group afterwards.
- The observation may be restricted to one specific element of the practice performance and therefore not require so much time and energy.
- The observation may alternatively be devoted to acquiring a rather comprehensive picture of the care provision in a practice and last for one whole day.

The following steps are taken in the practice observation.

Preparations

First of all definite arrangements should be made between the hosting practice and the observers with regard to various aspects of the observation:

- Agreement is needed with regard to the aspects of the practice performance which will be included in the observation: what is the observer going to evaluate, has the hosting practice any special request? In general the observation may address:
  - consultation skills: in this case the observer may be present in the consultation room or may review video or audio recordings, using for instance the instruments from Chapters 14 or 15;
  - clinical performance: using for instance the checklists from Chapter 16;
  - practice management: using for instance the instruments presented in Chapter 17.
- A timetable for the observation session is needed (see example).
- A suitable day or part of a day is selected when the practice is functioning at its normal routines and when sufficient patients are expected and sufficient diversity in practice activities will take place.

- Arrangements are made with regard to the feedback and discussion of this feedback: whether it will be written or oral, will take place between host and observer or with other practice staff involved in the discussion, or whether it will be presented during the meetings of the peer review group.
- At the beginning of the observation period, observers are introduced to all the staff and shown around in order to get overall familiarity with the practice.
- The hosting practice must clearly inform the patients about the observation (through the receptionist or through a clearly legible announcement in the waiting room). If the observer is sitting in on a consultation the GP must introduce the observer at the beginning of the consultation. The patient must be given the opportunity to refuse to allow the observer to be present (or to refuse the consultation to be recorded if that is the method being used).

Example: plan for a practice visit

The observation will include:

- an evaluation of general consultation skills;
- a patient survey with regard to the practice organization;
- inspection of the practice premises;
- questionnaires for doctors and other members of the practice team on the organization of services;
- a chart audit.

Time schedule:

8.00–8.30	General introductions, instructions with regard to questionnaires and patient survey.
8.30–9.30	Sitting in for observation of general consultation skills; patient survey.
9.30–10.30	Practice inspection; patient survey.
10.30–11.00	Coffee break.
11.00–12.30	Chart audit; continuation of the inspection; questionnaires for primary care team members.
12.30–13.00	Questionnaire for doctors; analysis of some of the data.
13.00–14.00	Lunch break; presentation of first impressions.
14.00–16.00	Analysis of the data; writing a report on the results.
16.00–17.00	Meeting with the doctors and primary care team members to discuss findings; make a plan with regard to desirable changes; agree further arrangements for the feedback report and discussion of the findings in the peer group.

This scheme can be restricted to half a day by excluding, for example, the observations in the consulting room or by writing the report and discussing the findings at a later date.

Observing practice and collecting data

The observers must gather sufficient information about the topics being reviewed to be able to achieve a valid evaluation. During an observation session like this, so much happens in such a short time, that it is difficult to get a complete picture. This is particularly the case when observing contacts between care providers and patients. Observers may become overwhelmed and confused by all the information and evidence that they are bombarded with. Therefore it is important:

- to use structured checklists or recording forms:
- to restrict the observation time to the gathering of information and not to attempt any initial analysis.

The hosting practice tries, as far as possible, to carry on as normal. The observers do not interfere with the proceedings, do not comment on the activities, and restrict themselves to observing and recording. Observers, in other words, play a rather passive role.

The way in which the various aspects of the practice performance may be evaluated is described below. It is of course possible to use instruments and procedures from other sources or undertake just part of the available procedures. For many GPs it is difficult to leave their practice for a whole day, while going to another practice for half a day might be much more practicable.

Clinical performance

In order to evaluate the clinical work of a GP, the observer may make use of a checklist from Chapter 16 or of the open recording forms in Chapters 8 and 9. In particular, it makes sense to select a variety of frequently occurring conditions in general practice and bring checklists for these topics (for example, hypertension, diabetes, sore throat). During consultations, observers may restrict themselves to completing general recording forms, because it may be difficult to find the right checklist at any particular moment. Checklists should be completed right after a consultation when the memory is still fresh. It does not take more than a minute to complete them.

General consultation skills

In order to evaluate general consultation skills and the communication between a GP and a patient, the instruments in Chapters 14 and 15 may be used. It is not usually possible to evaluate all skills at the same time, so the skills are split up, for example:

- During the first half hour the observer may concentrate on the opening phase of the consultations.
- During the next period the phase of diagnosis, treatment, and patient education and advice is observed.
- Another period of time is devoted to the evaluation of structuring the consultations.
- etc.

It is very difficult to complete the instruments during the consultations, so the observer may just make notes of the contacts or of the specific phases of a contact. It again helps to complete the documentation as soon as possible after the consultation ends.

Observation in the consulting room

The role of the observer during contacts in the consulting room is non-participating. The observer, therefore, needs a position in the room that fits this role. A good place is out of the line of vision between patient and doctor, but in such a place that both doctor and patient can be seen (see Fig. 11.1).

Practice management

In order to evaluate the management of the practice, the observer may use the instruments presented in Chapter 17. Various aspects can be observed:

- equipment;
- delegation of tasks;
- team working;
- organization of services;
- clinical and administrative recording;
- management of quality assurance and improvement;
- time management.

Evaluating the data

When all the relevant or desired data have been collected, the findings are analysed before feedback can be presented. The analysis involves:

Clinical performance

The sheets and/or checklists are completed, and then studied rigorously by comparing the observed performance with the criteria in the checklists or other accepted criteria. An overview is made of:

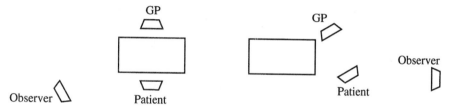

Fig. 11.1   Observation in the consulting room.

- actions performed according to criteria;
- recommended actions not performed;
- actions performed that are not recommended.

The observer produces an overview of the results, setting priorities. Were certain objectives well achieved? Were there important omissions in the clinical perform-ance? Were there particular areas where change would be especially beneficial?

General consultation skills

The complete instruments, as well as the verbatims of the consultations, are studied carefully. For each separate skill and/or phase in the consultation (structuring the consultation, managing the relation with the patient, general clinical and psycho-social performance, patient education, etc.) the routines of the GP are identified:

- What are the strong points in the performance?
- What aspects of the performance may be improved?

The feedback concerning general consultation skills generally will be largely qualitative in nature and will also be subjective to a certain extent. It is recommend-ed, therefore, to follow the guidelines in the instruments as closely as possible, in order to prevent 'labelling' and generalizations that can be over-critical.

Practice management

The data from questionnaires, the patient survey, inspections, and/or chart audit are analysed. The feedback contains factual information on these data. Because it is difficult to derive precise instruments for evaluating practice management criteria, observers may restrict themselves to giving feedback on aspects that seem to be remarkable, that are different from their own practice routines, or that are, in the eyes of the observer, suitable for improvement.

Giving feedback

Feedback may be given at various times during the observation, for example imme-diately after certain consultations. An advantage of this approach is that the experi-ence is very fresh, both for the observer and the host; but the disadvantage is that it may disturb the normal practice routines and that time for reflection on the feedback is not available.

A better approach is to give some impressions during coffee and lunch breaks. Those being observed can ask questions and may react to the feedback. The observers should emphasize that this feedback is derived from first impressions and preliminary.

It is important to give a formal verbal feedback before the end of the visit. Any visited practice will expect some kind of response at this stage and for observers to leave without some oral feedback will leave the host practice feeling 'flat'—and will miss the opportunity to receive the hosts' comments.

On the other hand impressions may still not be fully formulated—which may lead either to being over-critical or to being unduly complimentary, which may be embarrassing if the later written report is more critical. In order to achieve a constructive balance it is important *firstly* to emphasize that these impressions are early and not yet fully formulated and *secondly* to follow the standard procedure of emphasizing good points first, followed by areas where change may be indicated.

The feedback report

Ideally, a written report of the visit is made within a week or two of the event. This may be a time-consuming activity, but it is a very desirable and attractive way of rounding off the practice observation session. Those observed generally feel a great need for structured, well thought-out, differentiated feedback and also have the right to it. Writing such a report is very instructive for the observers. What's more, it gives them the opportunity to compare their own performance to that of a colleague in practice.

The feedback report should contain:

- positive points as well as possible gaps and things that may be improved;
- evaluations directed at routines in the practice and patterns in performance, rather than at specific observed cases.

The report may be *structured* in the following manner:

1. *General remarks*
   Subjective impressions from the observer about the running of the practice and about the practice culture (non-verbal aspects, attitude to practice work, etc.).
2. *Clinical performance*
   - an overview of the findings;
   - specific comments with regard to performance in relation to criteria.
3. *General consultation skills*
   - structuring the consultation;
   - managing the relation with the patient;
   - general somatic and psychosocial performance;
   - patient education.
4. *Practice management*
   - equipment;
   - delegation of tasks and teamwork;
   - organization of services;
   - recording;
   - quality assurance.
5. *Conclusions*
   - summary in which the most important good points and the most important recommendations for improvements are presented;
   - the observers' own learning points: things they found of great help and interest.

Of course, if the observation were restricted to certain aspects of the performance, then the report would contain only feedback on those aspects.

Planning and implementing changes

The results of the observation and the feedback may be discussed between the observers and the host practice team on the one hand, or in a peer group on the other. In both instances the following steps are taken:

- The observed GP and/or team reacts to the feedback: does it feel accurate? Which part of the feedback is and which is not acceptable?
- Next they select specific aspects that may be improved: a list is made of desirable changes in performance. These are then ranked according to their priority.
- Each of these possible changes is discussed: is change really possible? What are the consequences of making this change in terms of staff, time, money, education, etc.? What are the barriers to achieving the changes?
- Strategies for achieving the improvements are developed. A plan is made for working on the changes step by step: which aspect first, which next, where should the practice be a year after the observation?
- Finally, arrangements may be made for a follow-up visit, or for a review of change in the group.

To finish the quality improvement process, it is strongly recommended that the observed practice or GP formulates an explicit plan for change. This makes the activity considerably more valuable and it shows to the observers that their observations really contributed to improving patient care.

12 Structured peer group methods: quality circles, case analysis, and critical incident analysis

INTRODUCTION

In previous chapters some specific methods for peer review in a group of general practitioners or care providers in general practices have been presented in some detail. There are, of course, many other methods for peer review which may be very helpful in improving patient care. From the various methods we have selected three which will be described here briefly with some examples:

- Practice-based quality circle method: this is a structured group method, aimed at improving patient care and solving problems in general practice by involving all the relevant people related to a certain problem (GPs, staff, other care providers, patients, policy-makers).
- Case analysis: having chosen a topic for review, a case or cases related to that topic are discussed in a structured manner, with participants exchanging performance routines, giving each other feedback, and making plans for improving care on the subject.
- Critical incident analysis: a specific, not frequently occurring, but significant event or incident in a practice is analysed critically with the aim of carers supporting each other and learning how to prevent such an incident in the future.

These methods emphasize particularly the identification of problems in patient care and finding specific solutions for these problems. Measurement of the actual care gets less attention, and there is less emphasis on the setting of explicit guidelines or criteria. The methods provide a useful addition to those previously described, either as a warming up for peer group audit (for example, the case analysis), as a method to solve specific problems (quality circle), or to prevent very undesirable events in care provision (critical incident analysis).

THE QUALITY CIRCLE METHOD

A special type of peer review, in which people outside the practice team (for example, specialists, patients, other care providers, managers) may also take part is the so-called 'quality circle'. Experience with the methodology has been gained particularly in Belgian general practice (Schillemans *et al.* 1989), although it is also becoming more and more popular in other countries. The description of the method here has been mainly borrowed from the work of Schillemans and colleagues.

The quality circle was developed in the USA for application mainly in industry, in public services, and in some hospitals. The most important feature of the quality circle is that problem-solving, quality improvement, and decision-making are moved to the shopfloor. The care providers collaborate on identifying, analysing, and solving important problems related to their daily work. All those involved in the provision of a certain aspect of care come together on a regular basis to analyse and evaluate their activities. In this way, the evaluation is made an integral part of the intervention process, not a separate assessment activity. The emphasis of the quality circle, as far as peer review is concerned, is on identifying and delineating relevant problems and incidents in general practice care and developing and implementing a plan directed at solving these problems.

Experience in Belgium with quality circles in general practice has disclosed various advantages and limitations of the method. One strength is that patients and other parties may be intimately involved in the evaluation and improvement of care. However, it is a rather time-consuming activity for the participants, it demands well-trained circle leaders and interested patients. On the other hand, the method may be integrated in the peer review process described in the previous chapters. In particular, the method structures the process of selecting and demarcating relevant problems in practice and may support the effective implementation of desirable changes.

Each circle follows some basic principles:

- It is small and meets at regular intervals for a certain period of time.
- The composition of the group depends on the problem; different problems may require different group participation; care providers as well as patients can take part.
- Everyone involved in a certain problem participates in the circle—or at least a representative of each discipline involved.
- Participation is on the basis of equality.
- Discussion is directed at aspects of care that can actually be influenced or improved.
- All participants provide materials to support the process.
- The circle is supervised by a skilled supervisor, who has group leader skills.

The actual work starts with some *preparatory activities:*

- selection of a relevant aspect of general practice care for the quality circle;
- composing membership of the circle (doctors, nurses, patients, care providers, etc., depending on the theme);
- designing a plan for the circle (frequency of meetings, leadership, reports, etc.);
- during the first session the methodology is explained, as well as the aim of the circle; the expectations and motives of the participants are explored.

This preparation stage may require management participation to direct effort. Thus a group of individuals representing the main disciplines in the practice (a doctor, nurse manager, patient, etc.) may need to decide on the topic to be handled, and to compose the team to do the job. Without these two elements a quality circle can meander and waste time in deciding where to make its effort.

The quality circle method

1. Exchanging experiences
2. Structuring the subject
3. Defining and delineating the problem
4. Formulating goals
5. Choosing strategies and tools
6. Planning actions
7. Carrying out the planned actions
8. Evaluating the changes

An eight-step *procedure* is followed next (see box on p. 000).

1. Exchanging experiences

Participants start by presenting cases and specific experiences relating to the selected subject. Especial care must be taken to ensure patient anonymity and confidentiality in view of the extended nature of the group. Sufficient time is taken for these stories and for personal experiences. They should be as complete and detailed as possible. Group members listen carefully to each other's experiences and look for recurring elements in the stories. When necessary, additional data collection on the topic takes place (chart audit, patient survey, etc.).

2. Structuring the subject

In this step the ideas and experiences that come up again and again and that might be crucial for the selected subject are recorded. These ideas and experiences are structured, for example in the form of a herringbone or cause-and-effect diagram (Berwick *et al.* 1990); see example on the elderly (p. 92).

3. Defining and delineating the problem

The subjects which have been defined and structured in the previous steps are discussed:

- What is experienced as a problem?
- Who experiences this as a problem?
- Who can change the situation?

A detailed description of the real problem is made at this stage in order to prevent jumping too quickly to solutions. Inevitably the problem is defined against the background of certain expectations participants have with regard to the quality of patient care or of certain quality criteria they want to use. It is important to make these expectations and criteria explicit in order to arrive at a clear definition of the problem.

The quality circle cannot usually deal with every aspect of a problem in patient care. The crucial aspects have to be selected: aspects which have the greatest influence on the final outcome or aspects that are most crucial in terms of the values or expectations of the participants.

4.   Formulating goals

Once the participants have defined the problems, they have to determine whether they have enough information to deal with them. If not, specific data collection takes place in order to get more insight into the problems and their causes. If they do have a good understanding, then explicit goals for improvement are defined. Preferably only a few, realistic goals are selected.

Example: quality circle about 'the elderly'

A quality circle in a small village was composed of 3 GPs, 10 patients, 5 nurses, and 2 social workers. Representatives of local politicians were involved in the circle. The circle started with an exchange of 'classical problems of growing old' by all the participants. This resulted in a list of recurring themes such as fear, loneliness, how to get inexpensive help, activities in- and outdoors, losing power, adaptation of housing and living, security, decreasing financial security, meals, and personal hygiene. These themes were structured in the form of a 'herringbone diagram'.

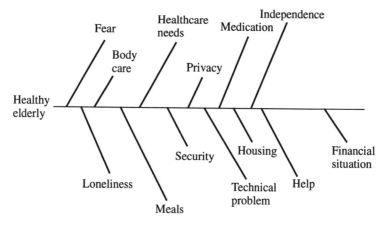

The circle selected as their main goal: improving security and housing, decreasing dependency on (healthcare) services, and improving the image of the elderly in the local community. Concrete interventions to achieve these goals concerned the development of a local centre, for a central telephone line staffed by elderly volunteers and political pressure to obtain better housing facilities. A delegation of the elderly contacted the local authorities and politicians and managed (partly due to new elections) to set up the new assistance structure and to acquire a budget for adaptation of 17 houses for elderly people per year. This quality circle was particularly successful, because of the clear view it had on the influence that a local group can have on local politics.

5. Choosing strategies and tools

This step begins by looking for as many suggestions and proposals for solutions and alternative ways of proceeding as possible ('brainstorming'). There should be room for creative thinking and for the consideration of all ideas, even if they seem unrealistic at first sight. The various ideas are written down and tested for effectiveness and feasibility. On the basis of this activity a strategy for bringing about changes is defined precisely.

6. Planning actions

Once the strategies have been selected a well-defined plan is drawn up. What steps have to be taken in order to bring about the desired change? Who is responsible for which action, when should the goals be achieved?

At this stage the quality circle can invite other persons to be involved or even set up a specific working party, responsible for implementation of the changes.

7. Carrying out the planned actions

Individual members of the circle, small working parties, or the whole circle ensure that the plans for change are carried out. Changes may concern the practice premises, the processes that care providers use in their care provision, teamwork between different care providers, or even changes with regard to processes in the community.

8. Evaluating the changes

The circle may end its activities by evaluating the new situation, after the change has been made. Has the situation improved? Were the goals attained? What part did the change strategy play in these improvements? When the changes have not been achieved, what was the cause of the failure? Can a revised strategy be developed which this time will be successful? And can the evaluation process be repeated again?

When the desired changes have been achieved, the circle has to decide:

- whether it will meet again after a protracted period in order to evaluate long-term outcomes;
- whether new topics will be addressed;
- whether it will end its activities.

Example: quality circle for diabetic care

The problem may be that only two-thirds of the diabetes patients in the practice have attended during the past year for diabetes control. The goal would be
to reach 100 per cent of patients. The quality circle might include doctor,
practice nurse, district nurse, receptionist, practice manager, two patients with
diabetes (one an attender, one a non-attender).

Cases might be described of regular attenders, and of non-attenders: in particular the patients might describe their benefits and problems with attendance.

Brainstorming would produce problems including: housebound patients,
transport problems, work conflict, difficulties making forward appointments,
problems with fasting, concurrent attendance at hospitals, fear of criticism,
feeling of lack of benefit, not wanting to bother doctor, denial, etc.

Positive solutions might include: visiting some patients at home, variable
clinic times, forward booking, reminder postcards, better patient education,
better information, a structured clinic protocol. Different members of the team
can be attributed responsibility for different areas—receptionist for appointments and reminders, district nurse to visit the housebound according to
receptionist's list, doctor/practice nurse to develop clinic protocols and patient
educational material, receptionist to run annual audit and point out patients
still defaulting to doctor/practice nurse.

Evaluation can be planned on the basis of an annual audit followed by an
educational meeting of the quality circle group.

It is important to take all the steps and complete the whole cycle. Sometimes this
may be difficult because the topic proves to be too difficult or not defined properly,
or the group composition presents some problems. In this case the group may go
back to management for reformulation of the task or the group; or it may itself
review the early stages in the process and try again.

CASE ANALYSIS

It may happen from time to time that information from the practice is not available
or difficult to gather, while there is still a need to work on a certain topic in a peer
review group. In this case a relevant case from daily practice may be selected or
prepared, which serves as a stimulus for exchange of routines, for comparing these
routines to guidelines, and for planning improvements in patient care.

The following steps need to be taken in undertaking case analysis:

1. Preparation

After having selected and defined a subject for the review one of the group
members selects a relevant case from his own practice. This case is written down

and structured along the headings of: history, examination, diagnosis, treatment, and education.

2.   Evaluation of routines

The group members start by elaborating the written case, step by step. They are instructed to write down their usual performance in comparable cases. When they have finished this task, there are two possibilities:

- The performance in the case is compared with certain guidelines or criteria for adequate performance; this can be carried out by the care providers themselves or by one of their colleagues.
- The performance in the case is compared with the performance of the colleagues in the group; for example one colleague analyses the performance or each group member presents their own performance in plenary.

From this activity some points for further discussion are selected: What are the most important differences in performance between the group members? Are these differences acceptable or not acceptable? Is it possible to formulate criteria for performance with regard to the key elements of the management of this particular complaint, disorder, or problem? Are these criteria realistic and feasible for practice or should they be adapted?

Steps in the case analysis

1. Preparation:
   - selecting a topic;
   - writing down a structured case.

2. Evaluation:
   - comparing with guidelines and/or exchanging usual routines;
   - feedback;
   - further discussion on the subject (guidelines, variation in routines).

3. Change:
   - identifying desirable changes and barriers to change;
   - defining strategies for implementing changes;
   - arrangements for follow-up.

---

3.   Change

Each individual group member selects a maximum of two important aspects of patient care that should be changed and considers whether there are specific barriers to achieving these changes. The participants next exchange this information. For each person a strategy for implementing the changes is discussed; participants support each other as well as possible. Finally it is agreed when the implementation of changes should be finished and a re-evaluation will take place. The arrangements for each individual in the group are written down in the peer review report.

CRITICAL INCIDENT ANALYSIS

A special example of case analysis is the so-called critical incident analysis. This is a structured peer review method aimed at discussing special events and situations in practice that are not frequently occurring, are very significant to the practice, and have given some problems to a specific care provider. It may be something that caused you pain and you prefer to sweep it under the carpet. Examples of critical incidents include missing the diagnosis of a serious condition; a patient complaining about a certain aspect of care provision; an unexpected situation during the weekend service; or conflict between a patient and a care provider.

A critical incident may begin by being the analysis of an apparently individual event—but as it is discussed it is often found that other similar episodes have occurred, and that a theme is apparent which can lead to improvement for future events.

Example: policy for anticoagulant therapy

A 58-year-old patient was admitted to hospital with a stroke. It was found that she had a frontal brain haemorrhage, and had been on anticoagulants for 15 years for a systolic murmur. The diagnosis had been made before the patient came to the practice and had not been reviewed.

The case was examined in all its aspects. Was anticoagulation control adequate? Was the indication for treatment well defined? Who was responsible for starting/stopping the treatment? How long should anticogulation be continued without review?

In the event there was no inadequacy found in the anticoagulant control for this case—but the grounds for anticoagulation were probably inadequate. It was then realized that none of the patients in the practice on anticoagulants had a written date for review or consideration of ending therapy. Thus this critical incident review of a woman who had a stroke ended with a new practice policy for recording anticoagulant therapy.

The method presented in this chapter is partly borrowed from van de Rijdt *et al.* (1988). The following steps need to be taken.

1. Preparation

A rigorous preparation is essential for dealing successfully with critical incidents. The group may arrange, during a meeting, that the next session will be devoted to critical incidents, and that two or three members will prepare this session. They each select an incident from their practice work that occurred not longer than about two months ago and they write down a short summary of the incident, according to the instructions given in the box.

Instructions for preparation of the critical incident method

- Select an incident that happened not longer than two months ago, that:
    - concerned an unexpected or difficult situation in practice;
    - or concerned a error or mistake in performance;
    - which is interesting for the whole group in order to improve patient care; refrain from telling tall stories!
- Write down a summary of the incident:
    - describe the background of the patient (medical history, other information);
    - present personal feelings about the situation;
    - present relevant diagnostic behaviour (history taking, examinations);
    - give information on the behaviour of the patient, also the non-verbal behaviour;
    - present the management of the problem.

---

2. Evaluation of care

During the session one or more incidents may be discussed, depending on the complexity of the cases and the number of participants who have prepared cases:

- One member presents his incident: factual information about background, medical history, personal feelings, diagnostic activities performed, and other relevant information with regard to the incident. No information is given about the management of the problem or the selected treatment. The other group members are allowed to ask questions about the background but discussion of management is not allowed.
- Next the participants write down for themselves, in one to two minutes, how they would have handled this particular case and they then compare their answers by going round quickly. The various ways of handling the incident may be entered on a flip-chart.
- Next the member who prepared the case introduces his performance in the specific incident and also the results and consequences of his solutions.
- The group then discusses the various solutions of the participants by comparing them and commenting on them. It is important to consider that there probably is not one best solution.

3. Change

The next step is identifying learning points. First the participant who brought the incident is asked to discuss what he or she has learned from this presentation and

---

Steps in the critical incident method

1. Preparation:
   - arrangements with regard to a session using the method;
   - two or three members prepare cases.

2. Evaluation:
   - one member presents a case;
   - others members ask questions (facts!);
   - each member presents their way of handling the incident;
   - the case presenter describes his or her performance in the case;
   - the various solutions are compared and discussed.

3. Change:
   - the case presenter selects learning points;
   - the other group members select their learning points.

---

from the feedback. In particular, performance in comparable situations in the future is considered. Next the other participants present their conclusions and learning points.

It must be realized that critical incident analysis is perhaps the most threatening of all forms of audit. Often the presenter is revealing to the group a case where he/she may have failed to undertake certain actions which may have led to unfortunate results. These cases are often the very ones that we would like to forget as quickly as possible because they cause us pain—and here we are not only not forgetting but even presenting them for discussion. It requires a supporting group well used to the principles of non-threatening, confidential, and supportive group work.

13 Managing the peer review process

INTRODUCTION

The importance of adequate supervision of peer review has been pointed out earlier (Chapter 6). This supervision may be either recruited externally or taken on by one of the group members. This may take various forms:

- The practice team leader, or another interested care provider in a health centre, co-ordinates and chairs the peer review process.
- One of the members of a local general practitioner (GP) peer group co-ordinates and chairs the meetings.
- A local GP tutor is invited to start the peer review process and to guide the peer group for a while, till the group is able to continue without help.
- A professional 'consultant' or 'facilitator' is hired to help in setting up the peer review activities.

The supervisor will generally function as chair rather than as an active participant and will need to maintain some distance and keep the group process going, when necessary. This chapter includes some instructions for supervisors of peer review. It is recommended that training of peer group leaders is provided, as is currently done in countries like The Netherlands, Ireland, and Germany.

A distinction can also be made between a newly formed group of care providers in general practice (for example, a local or regional educational group) and an existing group (for example, a primary healthcare team in a medical centre who collaborate closely).

An existing group will have developed certain group habits. People know each other and react in certain automatic fashions to each other. These patterns are not easily changed. Various objectives may play a role in such groups, such as improving personal performance as well as improving group performance and achieving better collaboration. These objectives and the way meetings have proceeded till now should be discussed first. Also the existing problems in working together should be made explicit, as well as arrangements on how to improve the process.

The task of managing the peer review concerns several aspects:

- the attitude of the participants towards peer review in a group;
- establishing the value of criteria and guidelines;
- setting up a peer review programme;
- chairing the group process;
- the employment of a variety of review methodologies;
- the promotion of independent peer review.

ATTITUDE TOWARDS PEER REVIEW

General practitioners have different ideas and expectations regarding peer review. They may have different motivations. Peer review can only succeed if all participants are prepared to commit themselves sufficiently to the process. They should be willing (van de Rijdt *et al.* 1988);

- to attend all meetings;
- to collect data on practice performance;
- to participate in discussions bringing in their views and routines;
- to do homework;
- to take their turn in reporting the sessions.

Therefore, one of the tasks of the supervisor is to assess the expectations, fears, aversions and prejudices of the participants and to create a positive motivation with respect to active participation in the peer review. This may be encouraged in different ways.

Paying attention to group functioning

Participation in a group of colleagues may evoke fear at the beginning of the audit. It is therefore essential, especially in the initial phase, to establish a constructive, pleasant, and open atmosphere in the group. The climate during the first meetings is often decisive: either open, direct, and mutually supportive, or vague, defensive, and uncommitted. Supervisors may encourage the development of a good atmosphere in various ways: by setting an example in being open and vulnerable, for example by submitting data on their own performance; by offering a clear structure; and by leaving enough room in the programme for participants to get acquainted and relaxed.

Discussing expectations, fears and aversions

Right from the beginning there should be ample attention paid to the expectations, fears, and hesitations of the participants. They should be offered the opportunity to express their feelings, and these should not be dismissed or rationalized by the group. A questionnaire which helps to elicit the expectations and problems with regard to taking part is presented in Table 13.1. The participants should understand that their concerns and fears will be taken seriously. Again, later in the programme it can be worthwhile to acknowledge fears and concerns, especially when the group starts with the actual audit. The threat may again increase because at that time the ground rules in the group have to be set: how openly and directly may one criticize one another? How far is it necessary to defend oneself? Implicit rules on the manner of conduct often need to be made explicit at that stage.

The most important fears and concerns that may be encountered in peer review are:

- Fear of the unknown: uncertainty regarding the procedure during peer review, reluctance to participate in a group, uncertainty about the effects of partaking in audit (for example, fear for loss of present work satisfaction, due to loss of freedom or to breaching the *status quo*).

Table 13.1 *Expectations and problems with regard to taking part in peer review: a questionnaire for peer review groups*

	Fully agree	More or less agree	Not agree
By taking part in peer review I hope to get better contact with colleagues	0	0	0
By taking part in peer review I hope to identify gaps and shortcomings in my performance	0	0	0
The time, money, and energy that peer review costs are a problem	0	0	0
I have problems with the use of criteria and guidelines for practice performance	0	0	0
By taking part in peer review I hope to learn how to relate and communicate better with patients	0	0	0
I hope that the peer review will improve the collaboration in our group or centre	0	0	0
I don't like the idea of getting criticism on my practice routines	0	0	0
I am not convinced that the peer review is really useful and that I will profit from it	0	0	0
I take part in the peer review because this kind of activity is or will be compulsory	0	0	0
By taking part in the peer review I hope to improve my knowledge and skills	0	0	0
I find it difficult to criticize the performance of my colleagues	0	0	0
I do not like working in groups	0	0	0
I fear the consequences of peer review, the changes that have to be made in my practice performance	0	0	0
By taking part in peer review I can break through the daily grind of work	0	0	0

- Aversion to guidelines: dislike of complying with guidelines and criteria, of relinquishing freedom from obligations, doubt concerning the usefulness of complying with guidelines, or hesitations with regard to their possible optimal character.
- Difficulties with change: conviction that implementing change requires too much energy; fear that patients will become dissatisfied or that consultations will overrun.
- Practical objections: belief that the peer review costs too much time or money, or that it demands all sorts of practical arrangements.

Offering structure

Establishing a positive motivation, dispelling fears, and creating a safe climate may also be achieved by the supervisor by providing a clear structure for the group members. The satisfaction of the participants is directly related to the degree of structure in the audit process. People do not like chaos. The supervisor may help in different ways:

- by giving insight into the programme and the peer review procedures at the beginning; it should become clear what the objectives are and what the programme and the methodologies look like;
- by making agreements and rules regarding the giving and receiving of criticism and feedback (see Chapter 7);
- by using well-defined performance review methods, which are clearly understood by the group members.

ESTABLISHING THE VALUE OF CRITERIA AND GUIDELINES

A specific, frequently presented problem in peer review has to do with formulating and using explicit guidelines and criteria for appropriate performance in practice. A serious discussion on the benefits and standing of guidelines may be important at certain stages of the programme.

One must remember that directly or indirectly expressed aversions to guidelines for adequate care will always occur. Having often worked many years in isolation and in the absence of feedback on their style of working, the participants will each have developed their own guidelines for practice.

General practitioners accept that each can have their own way of tackling particular problems, and moreover they feel that they rarely make mistakes. As a result, becoming confronted with different 'truths' and having mistakes pointed out is not appreciated and often even denied.

In such a situation various reactions may be expected in the audit groups: 'Guidelines generally don't apply to everyday practice', 'Every patient is different and requires a different approach', 'My experience is that my way of doing things works, patients are pleased with it', 'What the guidelines say cannot be verified; who tells me that it is really better?' It is important to go into these opinions seriously and to discuss them in the group. Negative reactions are especially common when a sense of obligation emanates from the guidelines.

In every audit group the supervisor and the group will regularly have to dwell on subjects like: How strong is the evidence for the agreed criteria? How strongly do the participants believe in them? How much liberty does one have to keep or to ignore them? In many groups one notices during peer review a non-committal attitude that is very difficult to break down. The participants acknowledge deviations from the collective agreed criteria or targets, admit that performance is really undesirable, but are reluctant to draw conclusions. Colleagues in the group tend not to question each other on this, and may quickly accept that personal preferences differ and that everyone may continue to act according to that preference.

It is advisable to confront the participants regularly with their own opinions in this matter. What is the group aiming for? Is it merely personal reflection on one's performance? Is it only the exchange of personal experiences and preferences? Or does the finding of deviations from the accepted criteria or targets standards imply the need for corrections in procedures with the audit group acting as superintending body? In a discussion on the status of guidelines the following points may be submitted:

- In working as a GP and in mutual assessment one always uses guidelines and criteria. Many of these remain implicit, however. The employment of explicit guidelines improves the objectiveness of the peer review.
- Given that the nature of good general practice is still largely unknown, guidelines must be flexible. They will always be open to discussion and will have to be adapted to new insights continuously.
- Guidelines represent an optimal situation. It is not intended that everyone (immediately) works according to this optimum, but rather that it serves to indicate the direction in which change is desirable.
- The guidelines should not be a straitjacket. Guidelines should leave room for a personal style and for some variation on the basis of foreknowledge of patients or the specific situation.
- However, the agreed guidelines and criteria do require a commitment. They are often upheld by literature, consensus discussions, or arrangements in the group. They are meant to reflect the current state of general practice knowledge. Deviation from these guidelines must be supported with clear arguments if the peer review is not to become a farce! At some point in the process of peer review the group will have to choose: will it continue in the main to exchange personal experiences or will the criteria also be employed as measuring rod, as a standard, with respect to which deviations need be justified?
- Evaluations in many groups show that the latter approach improves the group process and satisfaction with the audit.

SETTING UP A PEER REVIEW PROGRAMME

An important task for the supervisor is setting up a programme for the peer review process together with the participants. When the programme has been made beforehand by the supervisor as the initiator of the peer review, an extensive explanation of the goals and content of the programme is required, and the participants should be offered the chance to adjust the programme.

When an existing group with a group member as chair starts with peer review the task of the supervisor is helping the members to develop an interesting programme for a protracted period of time (for example, six months to a year). The programme is set up so that it gradually works towards increasing experience with the methodology, towards change and improvement in practice, and towards autonomy of the group (see box on p. 104, also Chapter 7, Table 7.1). The emphasis in the first session is on creating a safe climate and a positive attitude in the participants towards the peer review activities. They have to learn some review skills and acquire their first experiences with peer review. This may be achieved by applying simple, easy to perform exercises. (For example see Fig. 13.1.)

Next various methods for peer review considering various topics from general practice are practised. This offers the participants also the opportunity to evaluate each other's work critically and become aware of existing shortcomings.

Structure for a peer review programme of a beginning group

Introduction
- establishing conditions (safe climate, positive attitude);
- information on the content of programme;
- learning some basic skills;
- first experience with peer review.

Peer review skills
- experience with various topics and various methods of peer review;
- starting a process of improving practice performance.

Improvement of care
- emphasis on objectives for change and on evaluating progress;
- further experience with methods;
- increasing autonomy for the group.

Autonomy
- group functions without external supervision, group members chair sessions.

Which facilities are available in your practice and which routines do you use with regard to the care for diabetes type II patients?

Diabetes population well known or easily traceable (from record system)	0
Separate chart for diabetes patients	0
Blood glucose meter available	0
Surveillance system for diabetes patients	0
Reminders when patients do not attend appointments	0
Central role for the practice nurse in diabetes care	0
Check-up every third month	0
Treatment primarily directed to reducing weight	0
Blood pressure control annually	0
Inspection of feet annually	0
Examination of the eyes annually	0
Use of dietician	0
Quetelet-scale (body-mass index, BMI) is used	0
Firm appointment for the next check-up	0

Fig. 13.1   Routines in diabetes care (checklist)

Gradually, the emphasis shifts towards changing and improving performance in practice. The participants may become more demanding towards each other and set their goals a little higher.

Finally, the supervisor starts working on autonomy for the group; working towards a situation in which various group members chair the sessions and the group as a whole accepts the responsibility for the smooth running of the programme.

CHAIRING THE GROUP PROCESS

Another important task for the supervisor is chairing the group process and the discussions. One has to take care that the group starts and ends at the arranged time and that the agreed activities are performed in an orderly fashion. This includes for example (van de Rijdt *et al.* 1988):

- stimulating all the participants to become involved in the activities and discussions;
- bringing the group back to the subject at hand, when they lose the thread;
- summarizing the discussion or the views from time to time;
- making proposals for new activites;
- structuring discussions;
- persisting in questioning, when vague and unclear information is given;
- clarifying and emphasizing, when vague and unclear information is given;
- taking care that clear arrangements for the next sessions are made;

Generally, group members prefer firm and decisive group leadership. They tend to be annoyed or dissatisfied when the meetings end late, a meeting proceeds in a chaotic fashion, when people do not listen to each other, or when the objectives for the meeting are not achieved.

THE EMPLOYMENT OF A VARIETY OF REVIEW METHODOLOGIES

One of the goals of a peer review activity is to teach the participants a number of quality assessment and improvement skills. The group members should become sufficiently familiar with the methodology that they apply it as a matter of course, possibly without supervision later on. The skills the participants have to acquire are:

- selecting suitable problems for peer review;
- handling guidelines and criteria;
- setting objectives for improvement of performance;
- applying methods for collecting and analysing data;
- giving and receiving adequate feedback;
- constructively discussing in the group;
- developing and implementing plans for change.

The supervisor may achieve these goals as follows:

- By introducing and implementing the review methodologies and procedures in this book. At the beginning this may be done in a somewhat didactic fashion.

Together with the group the methodology is applied step by step so that the members gradually become acquainted with the procedures.

- By introducing variety in the peer review methods. In order to keep up motivation, most groups feel the need from time to time to work on a variety of subjects in the field of general practice, and to use various methods in doing so. Clinical performance, consultation skills, and practice management should ideally be reviewed in turn.

In this connection the developing of a process of change in the participants merits special attention. The ultimate goal of peer review is the improvement of general practice care for patients. It is frustrating to identify weak spots in personal or practice performance without trying to repair them. A peer review programme must therefore initiate a learning and transformation process in the participants. The programme, the audit group, and the supervisor should support individual participants in becoming aware of and accepting gaps in performance and should stimulate them to search for and experiment with alternatives. In this context it is important for the supervisor:

- to ensure that the auditee receives fair, well-based and relevant criticism. The supervisor should instruct the group in the giving and receiving of feedback, and set an example of fair criticism; only criticism that offers auditees insight into their routines and their flaws provides a basis for change;
- to help the auditee or the practice in selecting a number of specific areas for change, and in developing a firm plan for implementing that change in practice;
- to discuss any concerns that the auditee may have with regard to effecting changes, such as the attitudes of partners, or the time required;
- to keep an eye on the learning and change process. Of course, auditees are in the first place responsible themselve for watching over the process, for example by means of a report on the progress of change. However, the supervisor may also take note of the objectives and during a subsequent audit of the same GP the notes can be used to check whether the auditee has or has not attained the objectives of the change programme. The supervisor may then review with the participants the problems involved in realizing improvements in performance.

PROMOTING INDEPENDENT PEER REVIEW

Finally, a peer review group may have as its goal the initiation of a longer-lasting development and the fostering of continuity in the group. In this the supervisor must discourage dependence on supervision and stimulate the autonomy of the participants. This responsibility may give rise to a dilemma that is difficult to solve. On the one hand, an efficient and effective peer review process—much appreciated by the participants—requires active involvement of the supervisor. On the other hand, the need for autonomy of the group demands a discreet attitude. When the supervisor is actively involved the group members may be very enthusiastic about the audit, but it may also lead to them sitting and waiting increasingly for contribution of the supervisor. To avoid this dilemma the supervisor may act as follows:

- Make clear from the beginning that it is intended that the supervision is decreased gradually and that the group members take over the responsibility more and more. The importance of continuous audit is emphasized and explained: changes and improvements are often achieved only in the long run; the general practice field is very wide, which means that there are many areas in which critical audit is useful and that much time is required to cover all those areas; and audit should not be a once-only event, but should be included as regular activity in the normal work routine.
- At the end of every meeting the group may discuss the role of the supervisor during that meeting, as well as the extent to which the group has succeeded in becoming independent.
- Reflecting on any instances of passivity and dependence of the group on guidance may be a way of introducing a discussion about the independent working of the group.
- Move from a didactic method and from giving examples—for instance in giving and receiving criticism—to a method by which the group proceeds, and the leader only comments afterwards on the way in which the group performed.
- Following the introduction of a review method, its implementation is quickly handed over to the group itself. The group itself may give structure to the meeting, ensure that everyone contributes, cut short the discussion when it wanders off, and maintain the correct sequence of steps. The supervisor may intervene when anything goes wrong, or comment on the meeting and offer suggestions for improvement afterwards.
- Be a guide, not a leader!

Part III

Instruments for peer review

> The most basic of management principles state that the standards by which we judge performance should be clear, explicit and available for all to see.
>
> Lomas (1990)

INTRODUCTION

Explicit guidelines and criteria are of great help to care providers during peer review (see Chapter 2). They indicate the areas for improvement and change. They help care providers to become aware of existing practice routines. In this section of the book instruments for review of various important aspects of general practice care are presented. They are based on criteria which have been developed from rigorous analysis of the literature and consensus procedures, carried out by experienced general practitioners.

The instruments in these chapters are meant as tools in peer review. The criteria presented in the instruments are recommendations, not to be used inflexibly.
   They are meant to be used for:

- *developing local or practice-based objectives for improvement in performance;*
- *evaluating patient care, exchanging experience, and agreeing desirable changes.*

They are meant to be a support for the peer review activities described in this book. It is not possible to give a comprehensive overview of relevant instruments for all aspects of general practice care, so we present a selection which may be seen as examples. Instruments, guidelines, criteria from other sources may be used as well.

Instruments for evaluation are presented for four important aspects of day-to-day care in general practice:

- General consultation skills: A distinction is made between four basic skills:
    - structuring the consultation;
    - managing the doctor–patient relationship;
    - clinical performance;
    - psychosocial action.
- Patient education: the giving of information and instruction to patients. This instrument is an elaboration and refinement of the instrument for review of general consultation skills.
- Clinical performance: checklists are offered for review of the management of common complaints and disorders in general practice (for example, sore throat, diabetes check-up, hypertension, urinary tract infection).
- Practice management: various aspects of the organization of patient care are considered, including:
    - equipment;
    - teamwork;
    - services offered;
    - medical records;
    - quality management;
    - health education.

The reader is recommended to study and discuss a chapter first before using the instruments in the peer review process. It is also recommended that the criteria be adapted to the reader's own work setting.

14 Instruments for review of general consultation skills

INTRODUCTION

To perform adequately in patient care general practitioners need a method of problem-solving which is adapted to the specific features of their particular general practice. This style of problem-solving is noticeable particularly in the management of the contacts with patients. The handling of consultations is a central aspect of general practice which may be viewed from two perspectives. In the first place performance in specific cases with specific complaints and disorders may be evaluated: what should a GP ask, examine, prescribe when confronted with a patient with a sore throat (see Chapter 16)? Secondly it is necessary to evaluate the regular patterns of behaviour in contacts with patients, irrespective of the specific complaint or disorder. The criteria and instruments in this chapter are concerned with this second aspect of practice performance, the general consultation routines and skills of GPs. They are based on the theory as described in the book *To heal or to harm* (Grol 1988). A basic tenet is that GPs should avoid missing areas of care (for example, neglecting important medical and psychosocial aspects), but also avoid undertaking unnecessary actions.

FOUR BASIC CONSULTATION SKILLS

We work on the assumption that four basic consultation skills are central for the adequate general practice care of patients. Although they overlap one another a little, they each cover a fundamental part of the doctors' performance.

- *Structuring the consultation*. Each contact with a patient can be seen as a 'problem-solving process', a set of activities with the aim of arriving at a decision which is as well grounded as possible. In order to achieve this it is necessary to structure the contact methodically.
- *Managing the doctor–patient relationship*. This skill is concerned with the creation of a working, open relationship with the patient in which the patient feels secure, and in which both, as equal partners, take their part of the responsibility. The patient is encouraged to think about what is wrong and what should be done about the complaints or problems, whilst the doctor takes care of the clear explanation and information.
- *Clinical performance*. This involves both diagnosis and treatment, and the doctor should avoid inadequate or excessive help. The GP, in solving problems,

should use general practice epidemiology as a basis for deciding on the need for further examinations, therapy, and referral.

- *Psychosocial action.* The GP should be open to investigating the non-somatic side of the patient's complaint, paying attention to the psychosocial aspects, thus avoiding exclusively somatic attention to the complaints.

There is always going to be some overlap between these four skills. One should not regard the division as absolute, but as a framework for analysis: four ways of approaching the same behaviour. Moreover the term 'skill' is only partially accurate. Each of the four contains aspects involving knowledge, skills, and attitudes or values. To acquire good 'consultation skills' requires both knowledge and correct values.

THE STAGES OF THE CONSULTATION PROCESS

It is possible to define, for each consultation, stages or steps which must be taken to ensure adequate care. Each of the stages imposes its own demands on the carer's performance, in other words, demands certain skills. Broadly speaking, one can differentiate between activities aimed at clarification and those aimed at change (see Table 14.1).

Within these two activities a number of distinct steps can be defined: exploring the problems, clarifying the problem, defining the problem, discussing and formulating a plan, and evaluation of the consultation (see Figure 14.1).

Table 14.1　*The stages in a consultation*

Type of activity	Stages in the consultation process
Activities seeking clarification: Why has the patient come? How is the problem evaluated?	1. Exploring the problem: general exploration of the complaints and problems, both somatic and non-somatic, and clarification of the patient's expectations 2. Clarifying the problem: systematic collection of information through history taking, gathering psychosocial information, physical or other examination 3. Defining the problem: a clear summary of the problem; a preliminary or definitive conclusion about the nature, causes, and consequences of the complaints or problems
Activities aimed at change: What should be done about the complaint or problem?	4. Discussing a plan for management: discussing options for reducing, changing, or further clarifying the complaints or problems 5. Formulating a plan: formulating a policy and stating the actions required (treatment, medication, referral) 6. Evaluating the consultation: testing the effectiveness of the care provided

Name:
Group:

Date:
Assessor:

0 = action *not* performed according to criterion
1 = action performed *more or less* according to criterion
2 = action *completely* performed according to criterion
9 = not applicable or not assessable

	Structuring the consultation	Managing the doctor–patient relation	Clinical performance	Psychosocial action
Exploring the problem	☐ 1. Global orientation	☐ 11. Creating a relaxed and safe climate	☐ 22. Global exploration of complaints	☐ 33. Attention to patient's perception of complaints
	☐ 2. Building on previous contacts*	☐ 12. Open attitude, taking the patient seriously	☐ 23. Discussing self-care and other care providers	☐ 34. Discussing reaction of family, friends, colleagues to complaints
	☐ 3. Identifying and checking patient expectations	☐ 13. Stimulating patient's involvement in exploring the problem	☐ 24. Discussing effects of ongoing treatment, compliance*	☐ 35. Discussing effects of ongoing treatment*
	☐ 4. Formulating a working plan for the consultation	☐ 14. Interest in patient's life events		
Clarifying problem	☐ 5. In case of more than one problem: working in orderly fashion*	☐ 15. Stimulating active contribution of patient to diagnostic process	☐ 25. Diagnostic approach based on GP epidemiology	☐ 36. In case of psychosocial 'signals': further analysis*
	☐ 6. First history, then examination*	☐ 16. Explaining own thought process and diagnostic intentions	☐ 26. Preventive approach in diagnostic process	☐ 37. Discussing the relation between somatic and psychosocial aspects of problem*

Defining the problem	☐ 7. Explicit summary of conclusions, marking a new stage in the consultation	☐ 17. Giving understandable and complete explanation of problem ☐ 18. Discussing the explanation with the patient	☐ 27. Medical information on diagnosis and findings ☐ 28. Medical information on prognosis and course of problem	☐ 38. Information on psychosocial aspects of problem*
Formulating a plan	☐ 8. Explicit plan for further actions ☐ 9. Plan for evaluating the effect of treatment ☐ 10. Evaluation of the consultation	☐ 19. Exploring patient's views on policies/treatment ☐ 20. Understandable information and instruction on treatment ☐ 21. Discussing the treatment: agreement and feasibility	☐ 29. Simple solutions for treatment ☐ 30. Medical information on medication or referral ☐ 31. Health promotion ☐ 32. Follow-up arrangements	☐ 39. Psychosocial aspects involved in management plan* ☐ 40. Attention to self-responsibility of patients*
Strong and weak points				

Fig. 14.1 Frame for review of general consultation skills.

INSTRUMENTS FOR USE IN EVALUATING CONSULTATIONS

Figure 14.1 presents a framework for evaluating general consultation skills. Forty criteria are ordered according to the four basic skills on the one hand and according to the stages in a consultation on the other. Some criteria show an asterisk (*), which means that they are only applicable under certain conditions. For instance, discussing previous contacts concerning a problem is not possible when the consultation is for a newly presented problem.

It is difficult to score all 40 aspects of a consultation at the same time. It is recommended that the peer review process is focused at any one time on certain skills or certain stages of the consultation. However, if several different assessors are working together, they may concentrate on different criteria, in order to provide a comprehensive view of a GP's skills.

The guidelines in this chapter have been tested in several research projects. In the first place, the extent to which the instrument reflects the fundamental skills of general practice (content validity) has been evaluated. The guidelines have been carefully developed on the basis of literature, and consensus discussions have been held with a large group of experienced GPs and social scientists who are well acquainted with GPs' work. The aspects that are assessed are also found in other important publications in the field of general practice (for example, Pendleton *et al.* 1984; Royal College of General Practitioners 1985). Hundreds of experienced GPs, participating in peer review activities and using these guidelines, have in general found them relevant to daily work and feasible for peer review.

Consultation skills as evaluated using these criteria are strongly associated with clinical performance (guidelines in Chapter 16), with prescription and referral routines and with desirable attitudes in GPs. Doctors just commencing their vocational training have scored lower on the guidelines than doctors at the end of their GP training and experienced GPs, so the guidelines are capable of discriminating the degree of experience in the skills measured.

The reliability of the instrument in assessment of GPs' performance measured in various studies has been acceptable, but not impressive. It has to be accepted that a certain degree of subjectivity is inevitable in using these criteria, given the complexity of general practice work. Applying the criteria in standardized situations (for example, in a skills training) yields more positive results as far as reliability for assessment is concerned. However, when used for peer review activities, two or three consultations may show important learning points, and a high level of reliability and reproducibility is not critical.

STRUCTURING THE CONSULTATION

In assessing this skill attention is not particularly directed to the *content* of the consultation. Rather, what is evaluated is whether the various items and phases *occur in a logical sequence.* (See Fig. 14.2.)

	Name: Group:						Date: Assessor:				

0 = action *not* performed according to criterion
1 = action performed *more or less* according to criterion
2 = action *completely* performed according to criterion
9 = not applicable

		Consultation				
		1	2	3	4	5
1.	Global orientation					
2.	Building on previous contacts*					
3.	Identifying and checking patient expectations					
4.	Formulating a working plan for the consultation					
5.	In case of more than one problem: working in an orderly fashion*					
6.	First history, than examination*					
7.	Explicit summary of conclusions, marking a new step					
8.	Explicit plans for further actions					
9.	Plan for evaluating the effect of treatment					
10.	Evaluation of the consultation					

Fig. 14.2   Checklist for review of structuring the consultation.

Exploring the problem

1. *Global orientation.* The doctor actively tries to obtain a first impression of what is the matter, and what the patient feels about the complaints. It is more than an opening statement like 'Tell me, what brings you here?' The doctor will use open questions to encourage the patient's elaboration of the problem, and will also check for other problems that the patient may wish to bring up.
2. *Building on previous contacts.** If there have been earlier contacts for the presenting problem, the doctor refers to those earlier contacts, if necessary making use of background knowledge and the patient's record.
3. *Identifying and checking patient's expectations.* The doctor seeks explicitly to identify the patient's wishes and expectations, and, by posing open questions, tries to identify the reason for encounter and the help desired. As part of the conclusion of the initial phase, the general practitioner offers a clear summary of the needs of the patient, checking with the patient that it is correct.
4. *Formulating a working plan for the consultation.* The doctor tells the patient what the remainder of the consultation will consist of, explaining as clearly as possible the succession of steps to be taken.

Clarifying the problem

5. *In case of more than one problem: working in an orderly fashion.** The doctor him- or herself structures the consultation when various complaints or requests are presented.

6. *First history, then examination.** The doctor first takes the somatic and/or psychosocial history, and on the basis of this performs the examination.

Defining the problem

7. *Explicit summary of conclusions, marking a new stage in the consultation.* The doctor indicates the end of the information-gathering process by summarizing the analysis of the problem. What is assessed is whether this conclusion is formulated; its quality is not considered at this stage.

Formulating a plan

8. *Explicit plan for further action.* The doctor sets out an explicit plan for managing the problem, specifying who will undertake what and when.
9. *Plan for evaluating the effect of treatment.* The doctor clearly indicates how the patient should interpret the further course of the complaint, and if necessary, what to do next. This should include: if and when the patient should return for a control visit; what the patient should do if the complaints do not improve; a prognosis as to the duration of the complaint; some indication of the expected course of the complaint. For the purposes of assessment it is immaterial whether the information given is correct or not.
10. *Evaluation of the consultation.* The doctor checks *explicitly* whether the patient is satisfied with the consultation. Preferably this means checking on the patient's agreement with the plan of management.

MANAGING THE PATIENT–DOCTOR RELATIONSHIP

For the assessment of this skill, it is necessary not only to observe *if* a particular action is undertaken, but also, and especially, *how* the doctor relates to the patient. Note especially pauses, intonation, stimulation by means of open questions, the giving of impressions and information, and the expression of personal feelings. It is inevitable that a certain subjectivity of the assessor plays a part. Moreover, general practitioners have different personal working styles. But the idea is to audit as objectively as possible on the basis of concrete actions, taking into account the personal working style. Assessing the personality of the general practitioner is avoided as much as possible. (See Fig. 14.3.)

Exploring the problem

11. *Creating a relaxed, safe climate.* The doctor reassures the patient at the beginning of the encounter (verbally and/or non-verbally) and establishes an open and safe climate.

Name: Group:					
Date: Assessor:					

0 = action *not* performed according to criterion
1 = action performed *more or less* according to criterion
2 = action *completely* performed according to criterion
9 = not applicable

	Consultation				
	1	2	3	4	5
11. Creating a relaxed and safe climate					
12. Open attitude, taking the patient seriously					
13. Stimulating the patient's involvement in exploring the problem					
14. Interest in patient's life events					
15. Stimulating active contribution of patient to diagnostic process					
16. Explaining own thought process and diagnostic intentions					
17. Giving understandable and complete explanation of problem					
18. Discussing the explanation of problem with the patient					
19. Exploring patient's views on policies/treatment					
20. Understandable information and instruction on treatment					
21. Discussing the treatment: agreement and feasibility					

Fig. 14.3   Checklist for review of managing the doctor–patient relationship.

12.   *Open attitude, taking the patient seriously.* The doctor demonstrates receptivity by taking a patient-centred attitude, by pauses, by brief encouragements, and by reflecting the patients' statements.

13.   *Stimulating patients' involvement in exploring the problem.* The doctor stimulates patients *actively* by asking about their experience of and thoughts concerning the complaints, as well as their expectations of the general practitioner.

14.   *Interest in patients' life events.* The general practitioner demonstrates an interested attitude not only in respect of the situation of the patients, but also with regard to events and circumstances not directly related to the complaint or request presented.

Clarifying the problem

15.   *Stimulating an active contribution of the patient in the diagnostic process.* The doctor continues to stimulate the patient to explore the problem, by using both open and specific questions about the patient's ideas concerning the nature, causes, diagnosis, course, and implications of the complaints.

16.   *Explaining own thought process and diagnostic intentions.* When a history is taken or an examination performed, the doctor regularly gives clear explanations as to his or her own thoughts, intentions, and actions.

Defining the problem

17. *Giving comprehensible and complete explanation of the problem.* The doctor tells the patient what, in his or her opinion, the matter is, and offers some explanation. This means that the doctor does more than merely announce the diagnosis. The explanation is direct, open, and comprehensible to the patient. It responds to the questions of the patient, and is free of medical jargon. Important information is repeated.

18. *Discussing the explanation with the patient.* The doctor checks *explicitly* whether the patient has understood the explanation, and gauges the reaction of the patient to the information. Any discrepancy between the ideas of the patient and the conclusions of the doctor are discussed openly.

Formulating a plan

19. *Exploring the patient's view on policies/treatment.* The doctor involves the patient in the discussion on what should be done about the complaints or problems. This may be by suggesting possible alternatives, summarizing pros and contras, and letting the patient—wherever possible—make the choice. Another approach is to ask the patient's opinion on the management planned by the doctor.

20. *Understandable information/instruction on treatment.* The doctor discusses the purpose of treatment or management and points out the importance of complying with agreements. The doctor explains what exactly is expected of the patient, and what the latter may expect. The explanation should be clear and comprehensible. Rather than global advice, the doctor should give specific instructions with respect to desired behaviour (for example, 'take an hour's rest every afternoon' instead of 'take it a bit easier').

21. *Discussing the treatment: agreement and feasibility.* If treatment has been decided on, the doctor asks patients *explicitly* if they have understood it, how they feels about it, and whether they agrees with it. If not, they discuss the matter. The doctor also discusses the *feasibility* of the advice and the treatment for patients. Any problems are discussed.

CLINICAL PERFORMANCE

The aim is to assess the overall clinical performance of the care provider. Of special importance is the extent to which behaviour is in conformity with the general practice setting; for instance using time and choosing simple solutions first. At a more detailed level somatic performance can be assessed by specific criteria or target standards (for example, use the checklists in Chapter16 as an additional tool). (See Fig. 14.4.)

	Consultation				
	1	2	3	4	5

Name: Date:
Group: Assessor:

0 = action *not* performed according to criterion
1 = action performed *more or less* according to criterion
2 = action *completely* performed according to criterion
9 = not applicable

22. Global exploration of complaints
23. Discussing self-care, other care providers
24. Discussing effects of ongoing treatment, compliance*
25. Diagnostic approach based on general practice epidemiology
26. Preventive approach in diagnostic process
27. Medical information on diagnosis and findings
28. Medical information on prognosis and course of the problem
29. Simple solutions for treatment
30. Medical information on medication or referral
31. Health promotion
32. Follow-up arrangements

Fig. 14.4 Checklist for review of general aspects of clinical performance.

Exploring the problem

22. *Global exploration of complaints.* The doctor asks the patient to describe the complaints, and enquires among other things after their *localization, severity,* and *course.*
23. *Discussing self-care, other care providers.* The doctor enquires about what patients may already have done about the complaint or problem themselves, and what the results were. This may concern self-medication or experiences with other care providers.
24. *Discussing effects of ongoing treatment, compliance.** In cases of ongoing treatment, the doctor enquires explicitly about the course of the complaint since the treatment was started, and about any difficulties that the patient may have encountered. The doctor also checks on patient compliance, especially when the treatment has shown no effect.

Clarifying the problem

25. *Diagnostic approach based on general practice epidemiology.* In taking the history and performing the examination the general practitioner assumes hypotheses that are most probable in the general practice setting, taking a selective approach, but also taking signs of serious disorders into account.
26. *Preventive approach in diagnostic process.* Wherever applicable, the general practitioner adopts a preventive and anticipatory strategy making selective use

of screening methods, for example taking the initiative, when appropriate, to raise subjects like blood pressure measurement, smoking, or the taking of a cervical smear.

Defining the problem

27. *Medical information on diagnosis and findings.* The general practitioner offers an adequate explanation about the findings, the diagnosis, and the possible causes. In general, merely giving a medical diagnosis is inadequate.
28. *Medical information on prognosis and course of the problem.* The doctor gives adequate information about the prognosis and the possible course of the complaints or disease.

Formulating a plan

29. *Simple solutions for treatment.* The general practitioner chooses simple solutions as much as possible, bearing in mind any adverse effects of the treatment as well as the natural course or spontaneous remission of the complaints.
30. *Medical information on medication or referral.** In the case of *medication* the general practitioner gives information about the nature of the medication, dosage, possible adverse effects, and frequency and length of course. In case of *referral* the general practitioner adequately discusses the purpose and procedure of the referral, so that the patient knows what to do and what to expect.
31. *Health promotion.* Wherever necessary or desired the doctor provides information about general health issues and/or preventive measures, for example, about risk factors such as smoking, alcohol abuse, stress, and obesity.
32. *Follow-up arrangements.* The general practitioner indicates explicitly after each contact if and when the patient should return.

PSYCHOSOCIAL PERFORMANCE

With respect to psychosocial performance, the aim is to assess *with respect to content* the attention that the general practitioner pays to the general functioning of the patient. The idea is not so much to look for 'psychosocial problems' as to pay attention to thoughts, experiences, and concerns that patients have in relation to their problems and the way in which their problems are managed.

This skill inevitably overlaps with the medical performance and the doctor/patient relationship. (See Fig. 14.5.)

Exploring the problem

33. *Attention to the patient's perception of the complaints.* The doctor actively examines fears or anxieties related to the complaint, and pays attention explicitly to the *consequences* of the complaint for the patient.

	Consultation				

Name: Date:
Group: Assessor:

0 = action *not* performed according to criterion
1 = action performed *more or less* according to criterion
2 = action *completely* performed according to criterion
9 = not applicable

	Consultation				
	1	2	3	4	5
33. Attention to patient's perception of the complaints					
34. Discussing reactions of family, friends, colleagues on complaints					
35. Discussing effects of ongoing treatment					
36. In case of psychosocial signals further analysis*					
37. Discussing the relationship between somatic and psychosocial aspects of the problem*					
38. Information on psychosocial aspects of the problem*					
39. Psychosocial aspects involved in management plan*					
40. Attention to self-responsibility of patient*					

Fig. 14.5   Checklist for review of general aspects of clinical performance.

34. *Discussing reactions of family, friends, and colleagues to complaints.* Are they aware of the problem, was the patient sent by them to the doctor, are they reinforcing the complaints or not taking them seriously?
35. *Discussing effects of ongoing treatment.** In case of a follow-up encounter the general practitioner examines the effect of earlier contacts on the patient's feelings or environment.

Clarifying the problem

36. *In case of psychosocial signals: further analysis.** This is only applicable where there is a clear psychosocial component in the initial phase. The doctor explores the psychosocial aspects and explores their significance in relation to the patient's complaints.
37. *Discussing the relationship between somatic and psychosocial aspects of the problem.** This only applies where there are clear psychosocial aspects. The doctor takes both the physical and the psychosocial side seriously, adopts a dual approach, and clarifies, wherever necessary, the relationship between physical complaints and psychosocial aspects.

Defining the problem

38. *Information on psychosocial aspects of the problem.** In providing explanation the doctor pays attention to the psychological and/or social aspects that play a part in the complaints or problems. The GP should clarify possible

associations, discuss the possible significance of psychosocial aspects in the complaint, and explain how this may influence the course of the complaint.

Formulating a plan

39. *Psychosocial aspects involved in management plan.** The doctor adopts a 'dual approach' with regard to management, paying attention to the physical side, but also discussing what should be done about the psychosocial aspects, for example in the form of a further talk or a referral.
40. *Attention to self-responsibility of patient.** If necessary, a concrete and feasible plan is made in which the self-motivation and responsibility of the patient are stressed (for example, assignments on which the patient can work).

15 Instruments for review of patient education

The giving of information to patients is a specific and very important aspect of the consultation process and one of the central tasks of the general practitioner. For this reason, skills described in a general fashion in the previous chapter are presented more extensively in this chapter.

Patient education in general practice is of great importance for various reasons:

1. Medico-technical function: for every cure the patient's contribution is mandatory. The patient must take drugs, adhere to regimens, or return for follow-up. Patients require information in order to understand why this is necessary and what exactly is expected of them.
2. Psychosocial function: being ill or having complaints, and visiting doctors or a hospital for tests or treatment, usually cause fear or worry. Information may dispel these feelings when it is given adequately.
3. Interpersonal function: the quality of the relationship between doctor and patient is partly determined by the transfer of information; inadequate or confusing information is often the cause of dissatisfaction with received care.
4. Economic function: patient education can improve the co-operation of the patient, improve treatment success, and reduce the professional contribution required, which may reduce costs.
5. Ethical function: patient education ensures that the patient is treated as an equal and co-responsible partner instead of as an object or 'case'.
6. Political function: not providing information is democratically undesirable.
7. Juridical function: patients have a lawful right to information; they should be able to decide on treatment and investigations on the basis of 'informed consent'.

It is apparent that different parties in healthcare consider patient education important for different reasons, and that they have different priorities. In a Delphi procedure in which GPs, representatives of patient organizations, and experts in health education sought consensus on the subject of patient education by the GP, it turned out that GPs emphasize in particular the medico-technical function, patients the interpersonal and ethical function, and health education experts the juridical function of patient education (Grol 1992*b*).

WHAT IS PATIENT EDUCATION?

Definitions of patient education are rather diverse. Often they are so comprehensive as to include the entire communication with the patient. Certainly it is clear that patient education by the GP can hardly be viewed in isolation from the rest of the consultation; they are, as it were, interwoven. An operational description is Bartlett's (1983), which distinguishes interpersonal skills, transfer of information, and motivating the patient to adhere to advice (Table 15.1).

- Interpersonal skills: establishing a confident relationship with the patient, putting the patient at ease, and being open to the patient's feelings, wishes, and ideas. This appears to be a necessary condition for effective patient education, especially with regard to the patient's confidence in the doctor and satisfaction with the provided care.
- Adequate transfer of information: explanation that is understandable, acceptable, correct with respect to content, and relevant to the patient's needs. This affects the patient's knowledge about the problem, insight into the required treatment, remembering of instructions, and dissipation of anxiety.
- Involvement of the patient in management: involving the wishes of the patient in deciding on the course of management, discussing the possible effects of a recommended treatment, and discussing the practicability of the advice in daily life. This appears to influence the readiness of the patient to adhere to advice and instructions.

IS PATIENT EDUCATION EFFECTIVE?

Patient education should contribute to patients gaining insight into their disease and the treatment which it requires. This should improve co-operation with the agreed course of management. In the end, it should result in maintenance or improvement of the health status. Numerous studies have indicated that patient education yields these effects. The following paragraph summarizes these studies (Grol 1992*b*).

Interpersonal skills

The relationship between a sympathetic and open attitude on the part of the GP and satisfaction of patients has been demonstrated convincingly in several studies

Table 15.1   *Patient education by the GP*

Performance of the GP	Short-term effects	Long-term effects
Good interpersonal, communication skills	Confidence, satisfaction	
Adequate transfer of information	Understanding, remembering, participating	Improved health status and illness behaviour
Involvement of the patient in management	Patient compliance	

(Kincey *et al.* 1975; Pendleton 1983). It has also been shown that more satisfied patients are more inclined to adhere to instructions; for instance, in compliance with drug prescriptions. On the other hand, brief and impersonal consultations, during which the expectations of the patient were not examined, turned out to have a deleterious effect on the illness behaviour. Moreover, the more doctor and patient succeed in sharing an understanding of the problem, the more the actual health status ameliorated. An improvement of the blood pressure was seen in patients who were able to express their worries and expectations during the consultation (Kaplan 1989).

Adequate transfer of information

The purpose of explanation is for the patient to gain adequate insight into the complaint or disease and the measures required for its alleviation. Much of the information given by doctors bypasses patients because they do not understand the terminology of the doctor or because they do not understand the information. In studies carried out by (Ley *et al.* 1976; Ley 1982) in general practice, it turned out that patients had not understood one-third to a half of all the information concerning the cause, diagnosis, prognosis, and the treatment. Indeed, patients proved to forget, on average, half of the information given. Ley's studies indicated that effective transfer of information means, among other things:

- categorizing information, providing a clear structure;
- repeating and summarizing;
- giving clear instructions for patient behaviour;
- giving important information first.

Supplementing oral explanation with written information improves the knowledge and the recall of the patient considerably. A meta-analysis of 61 studies (Hall *et al.* 1988; Roter 1989) showed that better transfer of information and a more co-operative relationship between doctor and patient resulted in improved recall of information.

Involving the patient in management

Finally, the GP should seek to ensure that the patient complies with the advice and instructions. Research has shown that patient compliance is often very much overestimated (Haynes *et al.* 1987; Meichenbaum and Turk 1987). Inadequate adherence appears to vary from 25 per cent (short-term medication), 50 per cent (protracted medication), 70 per cent (dietary advice), up to 90 per cent (advice to stop smoking) (Sackett and Snow 1979; Becker and Rosenstock 1989; Sackett 1985). The following measures have been shown to be effective in improving patient compliance:

- giving instructions that are as simple as possible: establishing priorities, keeping the number of drugs and the daily dose low (Becker 1985; Morris and Halperin 1979);

- checking non-compliance, for instance by counting tablets at follow-up consultations; concentrating on high-risk groups, and asking the patients if they sometimes slip up. The application of these measures has been shown to lead to a sizeable improvement in patient compliance (Wandless *et al.* 1979, Morisky *et al.* 1986);
- influencing the behaviour and habits of patients: fitting the therapy in with existing habits, arranging reminders, rewarding, etc. (Cameron and Best 1987; Kottke *et al.* 1988);
- involving others in the patient's environment in management (Becker and Green 1975).

CONSENSUS STUDY

With regard to patient education, different parties involved in healthcare propose different requirements and criteria that the GP should meet. The question remains as to how far all these recommendations are relevant to, and workable in a GP's practice. To answer this question a consensus study was held among GPs, patients, experts in health education, and policy-makers (Grol 1991).

In three rounds using written questionnaires, a Delphi panel of the participants reached consensus concerning which aspects of patient education should be present in every consultation, irrespective of the main complaint or disorder. The panel achieved agreement on 33 criteria for good patient education.

CRITERIA FOR PATIENT EDUCATION

As mentioned earlier, patient education is not an isolated part of the consultation with the GP, but is more or less interwoven with the whole consultation process. The instrument for peer review of patient education therefore consists of criteria arranged according to the four phases of the consultation: exploring the problem, clarifying the problem, defining the problem, and formulating a plan. The criteria are a refinement of those for general consultation skills (Chapter 14).

To aid in peer review, *checklists* are provided that permit rapid and efficient audit (Figs 15.1–15.4). The review may be done by a GP him/ herself or by a colleague observing in the consulting room or viewing/listening to a video- or audiotaped consultation. The entire list may be used or only a part of it (for example a particular phase). By auditing the patient education by a GP during more than one consultation, insight is rapidly achieved into the subject's regular routines and into skills in this area.

A score for the performance per consultation may be computed by adding up the items carried out and dividing this sum by the maximum number of applicable items. The score can also be determined over various consultations.

EXPLORING THE PROBLEM

Commentary

Both the consensus meeting and the study of the literature indicated that the crux of good patient education is a patient-centred approach during the initial part of the consultation. In this phase, the GP should take account of the following:

- What are the opinions and concerns of the patient?
- What are the patient's needs and expectations?
- What has the patient already done?
- What are the effects of any treatment in progress?
- Are there any problems with respect to compliance with prescriptions and advice?

A reason for encounter is then formulated together with the patient, and the GP explains how the problem will be addressed in the course of the consultation. (See Fig. 15.1.)

Criteria

1. *Find out the patient's ideas and concerns.* Examination of the ideas and concerns which the patient (or the patient's family) have with regard to the complaint or problem. ('What do you think is the matter?', 'What does this mean to you?')
2. *Find out what the patient has already done.* Ascertainment of what the patient has already done to alleviate the complaint or problem (rest, exercises, household remedies, self-medication, complementary medicine).

	1	2	3	4	5
Exploring the problem					
1. Find out the patient's ideas and concerns	0	0	0	0	0
2. Find out what the patient has already done	0	0	0	0	0
3. Identify the patient's needs and expectations	0	0	0	0	0
*4. In follow-up contacts: inquire about the effect of the treatment in progress	0	0	0	0	0
*5. In follow-up contacts: if advice is not followed or treatment is having no effect; discuss compliance problems	0	0	0	0	0
*6. In follow-up contacts: discuss possible resistance to regime	0	0	0	0	0
7. Formulate the reason for encounter or the help needed	0	0	0	0	0
8. Explain the further course of the consultation	0	0	0	0	0

Fig. 15.1   Checklist patient education: exploring the problem.
(o = act not performed; ● = act performed; ✗ = not applicable)

3. *Identify the patient's needs and expectations.* Exploration of what the patient needs and expects with regard to the complaint or problem (relief of worry, relief of pressure from the family, advice or treatment).

4. *In follow-up contacts: inquire about the effect of treatment.** In the case of follow-up contacts, a check on whether the agreements have been complied with, and what the effect of the treatment has been.

5. *In follow-up contacts: if advice is not followed or treatment is having no effect; discuss compliance problems.** When advice and/or agreements have not been complied with, or when the expected effect of a therapy fails to appear, consideration of what problems the patient may have encountered in adhering to the advice or agreement.

6. *In follow-up contacts: discuss possible resistance to regime.** If the patient has experienced difficulties or doubts with regard to the course of management previously agreed, it is necessary to discuss whether the patient still approves of the agreed goal of treatment or behavioural change, or whether that goal must be modified.

7. *Formulate the reason for encounter or the help needed.* In agreement with the patient a formulation of the key question or the key problem and needs of the patient in this contact.

8. *Explain the further course of the consultation.* An explanation of what will be the sequence of events in the contact with regard to both medico-technical and psychosocial aspects

CLARIFYING THE PROBLEM

Commentary

During the phase of problem clarification, the GP seeks by means of history and/or examination to elucidate what is exactly the matter. In order to secure satisfactory co-operation of the patient and to gather the data required to formulate a working hypothesis, the explanation offered during this phase is very important. Whether regarding physical examination or in taking a history, the more the patient knows about why things are being done, the greater will be the co-operation. (See Fig. 15.2.)

Criteria

9. *Explain any physical examination.** In the case of physical examination, an explanation (step by step) of what kind of examination will be performed.

10. *In case of unpleasant physical examination: ask about earlier experience and tell what to expect.** The GP enquires about earlier experience and explains, if necessary, what to expect (for example with rectal or vaginal examination, or examination of children).

11. *Discuss patient co-operation needed during examinations.** In case of examinations the GP discusses with the patient what is expected.

	1	2	3	4	5
Clarifing the problem					
*9. Explain any physical examination	0	0	0	0	0
*10. In case of unpleasant physical examination: ask about earlier experiences, tell what to expect	0	0	0	0	0
*11. Discuss patient co-operation needed during any examinations	0	0	0	0	0
*12. If examination meets with incomprehension or resistance: establish agreement	0	0	0	0	0
*13. Psychosocial problems: discuss which aspects should be talked through	0	0	0	0	0
14. Give preliminary conclusions	0	0	0	0	0

Fig. 15.2   Checklist patient education: clarifying the problem.
(o = act not performed; ● = act performed; ⊗ = not applicable)

12.   *If the prospect of examination meets with incomprehension or resistance: establish agreement.** If there is any indication of disinclination on the part of the patient concerning examination, the GP must establish the patient's explicit agreement.
13.   *Psychosocial problems: discuss which aspects should be talked through.** With psychosocial problems, patients should be informed and should agree on which aspects of a problem they wish to talk about further.
14.   *Give preliminary conclusions.* When taking a history, tentative conclusions should be offered as a first reaction to the questions, worries, concerns, and opinions of the patient.

DEFINING THE PROBLEM

Commentary

Patient education is of special significance during this phase, in which findings from the problem clarification stage are sorted out and ordered. The goals of education at this stage are firstly to offer the patient insight into the complaints or discomforts, and secondly to answer the questions with which the patient came to the consultation, and to dispel concern. Patient education should now address several important items:

● the findings of the examination;
● the nature of the disorder;
● the cause of the disorder;
● the seriousness of the disorder;

● the natural history/prognosis of the disorder.

The significance of each of these aspects will vary from one consultation to another but taken together they guarantee that the patient becomes properly informed. It is important that the explanation offered in these areas is concise and clear. It is also advisable to check whether the patient has understood the information, especially with complex problems. (See Fig. 15.3.)

Criteria

15. *Summarize the findings of the history and the examinations.* Discussion of the outcome of the history taking, the physical and the psychosocial examinations, and possible additional tests.
16. *Discuss the possible nature of the problem.* Discussion of the probable nature of the disorder or the problem, as well as any alternative diagnoses.
17. *Discuss possible explanations and causes.* Discussion of the likely physical and/or psychosocial explanation, or what the reason for its development or persistence are (for example, cough caused by smoking).
18. *Discuss the seriousness of the disorder.* Discussion of the seriousness of the disorder or the problem, including the degree of uncertainty.
19. *Discuss the expected course of the problem.* Discussion of the expected course of the complaint including the degree of uncertainty.
20. *In case of complex problems: sound out the need for further explanation.** In case of complex complaints or disorders: exploration of the need of the patient for further explanation and, if so desired, provision of such explanation.

	1	2	3	4	5
Defining the problem					
15. Summarize the findings of the history and examinations	0	0	0	0	0
16. Discuss the possible nature of the problem	0	0	0	0	0
17. Discuss the possible explanations and causes	0	0	0	0	0
18. Discuss the seriousness of the problem	0	0	0	0	0
19. Discuss the expected course of the disorder	0	0	0	0	0
*20. In case of complex problems: sound out the need for further explanation	0	0	0	0	0
*21. In case of doubt about being well understood: check the understanding of the explanation	0	0	0	0	0

Fig. 15.3   Checklist patient education: defining the problem.
(o = act not performed; ● = act performed; ⊠ = not applicable)

21. *In case of doubts about being well understood: check the understanding.**
     In case of a difficult problem or doubts about the patient's grasp of the expla-
     nation: explicit examination of how far the patient understood the information.

DISCUSSING AND FORMULATING A PLAN

Commentary

The patient education during the last phase of the consultation is especially intended to secure that the course of management decided on jointly by the GP
and the patient is indeed carried out as planned. In other words, that medication is
taken in accordance with the prescription, that the patient returns for a follow-up
visit at the time agreed on, that patients are well aware of what is expected of
them and what they may expect in case of referral, and that they use fully any
opportunity for self-help. Sometimes, when the course of management demands
much of the patient and affects the patient's life deeply, it will be necessary to
examine its feasibility. (See Fig. 15.4.)

		1	2	3	4	5
	Discussing and formulating a plan					
22.	Discuss the importance of the treatment	0	0	0	0	0
23.	In case of complex management plans: check feasibility	0	0	0	0	0
24.	Discuss possibilities for self-care	0	0	0	0	0
*25.	In case of medication: agree regime	0	0	0	0	0
*26.	In case of a special type of drug: explain or demonstrate how to use it	0	0	0	0	0
*27.	Medication: explain when effective and how long to continue	0	0	0	0	0
*28.	Medication: discuss consequences of over/underdosing	0	0	0	0	0
*29.	In case of possible serious side-effects of treatment: explain how to handle	0	0	0	0	0
*30.	In case of referral: discuss pros and cons	0	0	0	0	0
*31.	Referral: discuss patient's preferences	0	0	0	0	0
*32.	Referral: if possible, prepare patient	0	0	0	0	0
33.	Discuss follow-up arrangements	0	0	0	0	0

Fig. 15.4 Checklist patient education: discussing and formulating a plan.
(o = act not performed; ● = act performed; ⊠ = not applicable)

Criteria

22. *Discuss the importance of the treatment.* Indication of the importance or the necessity of the chosen course of treatment and of following the agreed prescription and advice.

23. *In case of complex management plans: check their feasibility.** If the management discussed is complicated or severely affects the patient's life pattern, it is necessary to establish whether the patient considers it feasible.

24. *Discuss possibilities for self-care.* If there are self-care possibilities, discussion of what patients may do themselves to further recovery.

25. *In case of medication: agree regime.** Discussion of which drugs are suitable, how often they should be taken, and when.

26. *In case of a special type of drug: explain or demonstrate how to use it.** In case of special forms of drugs (suppositories, eye drops, inhalers, etc.) explanation or demonstration of how the drug should be administered.

27. *Medication: explain when effective and how long to continue.* Explanation concerning when the medicine may be expected to become effective, and for how long it should be taken (for example, completing a course of antibiotics).

28. *Medication: discuss consequences of over/underdosing.** If there are adverse consequences associated with taking too much/too little of the drug or forgetting to take it, discussion of these consequences.

29. *In case of possible serious side-effects of treatment: explain how to handle.** If the possibility of side-effects is sizeable or the side-effects may have serious implications for the patient, discussion of possible side-effects and what to do if they occur.

30. *In case of referral: discuss advantages and disadvantages.**

31. *Referral: discuss patients' preferences.** Exploration of whether the patient has a preference, and subsequent agreement on the preferred referral.

32. *Referral: if possible prepare the patient.** In so far as possible, preparation of the patient (in general terms) for what will take place during examination or treatment elsewhere.

33. *Discuss follow-up arrangements.* Agreement concerning if and when the patient should return to see the GP.

16 Instruments for reviewing performance in common conditions

In this chapter we present checklists for reviewing the care of a number of clinical conditions. We trust that these can be used by practitioners as a basis for drawing up their own plans and for developing criteria and target standards against which their care can be evaluated.

It is not possible to develop one checklist which will suit all practitioners. We behave differently according to our own convictions, in response to differing environments, with differing populations and variable secondary care facilities. Local epidemiology, agreements between healthcare providers, expectations of the patient, medical culture, and personal preference may all influence the actions considered appropriate in specific cases. It usually saves a great deal of time, and avoids unforeseen omissions, to build on an external framework; but it is also important for a practice or group of general practitioners to develop a checklist for its own use, so the protocol becomes relevant to the local situation, and the practice develops 'ownership'.

Guidelines should as far as possible be supported by scientific evidence as being associated with beneficial outcomes. At present such evidence is scanty for much of general practice medicine. The checklists in this chapter have been drawn up after careful study of general practice literature, and then on the basis of discussions with experienced GPs; but research and new insights will make repeated changes necessary.

The checklists are presented with columns so that a consultation or situation can be reviewed for the inclusion of the various items. Practitioners will probably wish to vary the checklists to suit their own management protocols, and to change their criteria for evaluation as their own care plans develop. By setting themselves more rigorous criteria, and attaining them more frequently, practitioners will be improving their quality of care.

It must be emphasized that these checklists enable peer review groups to review their management of topics as part of discussion in the group. Variation in patients' symptoms will mean that all the items are rarely indicated for inclusion in a consultation. So the list should not be regarded as a test whereby ideal care can only be considered to have been delivered if all the items are 'ticked off'.

GENERAL PRINCIPLES

When drawing up the checklists a number of principles were followed (see also Grol 1988):

General practitioners should act in a systematic but selective fashion

Excessive attention to physical problems can cause patients to become dependent on the general practitioner and so be a barrier to their own problem-solving capacities. On the other hand, omitting to deal with somatic complaints can mean that the length of the illness is prolonged and confidence in the practitioner diminished. By working in a selective and systematic fashion, the general practitioner can reduce the chances of giving too much or too little care.

By selective and systematic is meant that a systematic review is carried out of the differential diagnostic possibilities of a complaint; but at the same time, the diagnostic information is collected selectively with a view to testing out relevant hypotheses only and not gathered for its own sake.

When clarifying the problem a systematic approach is especially important. At this stage the general practitioner is getting an idea of the circumstances that have played a part in the complaint arising and persisting, and in doing this, the general practitioner continually takes decisions on the basis of information collected already as to how to proceed in further information gathering. Knowledge of epidemiological likelihood, relevant background, and medical history of the patient and the diagnosis of psychosocial factors play an important role in this. In each decision the GP is faced with a dichotomy between doing too much or doing too little, and this is reflected in the contrast between working systematically and selectively. Working systematically demands a broad approach (open questions, listening to all information from the patient in an unbiased way, and being amenable to alternative explanations) whereas working selectively demands a doctor-directed amplification of specific differential diagnostic hypotheses.

On the other hand, the two principles also complement one another. The broad orientation attained by open questioning and listening produces global hypotheses which later through more selective questioning or examination are transformed into more specific hypotheses for testing out.

The clarification stage ends with the definition of the problem or the development of a diagnosis, which is an essential part of a systematic approach. The prognostic implications of a diagnosis lead on to management which is directed towards change.

Finally, we would point out that the method of work described here differs from the method of work used in specialist medicine, which aims at analysing the effects of all possible specific hypotheses systematically and extensively and is not a selective method of work. As Marinker (1990) has written, 'The task of the specialist is to reduce uncertainty, to pursue possibility, and to marginalise error. The task of the general practitioner is to accept uncertainty, to explore probability, and to marginalise danger'.

The general practitioner should keep the chance of damage to the patient as small as possible

At each stage a GP will consider critically the positive and negative consequences for the patient resulting from a certain decision. This requires a clear understanding of the range of normality, an appreciation of general practice epidemiology, and an understanding of the positive and negative predictive values of examinations and tests (for instance that only 3 per cent of 60-year-old men but 25 per cent of 60-year-old women have a cholesterol level of 8 mmol/l or above). Only in this way will the general practitioner be able to concentrate on findings of importance, while avoiding labelling as 'ill' patients whose findings and investigations are only randomly or mildly aberrant from normal.

The general practitioner should recognize that a great number of complaints are self-limiting

By unnecessarily treating these illnesses the general practitioner can contribute to a confirmation of the patient's sick role and thereby increase the risk of iatrogenic injury. Again, knowledge of epidemiology plays a great role (for instance, knowing the epidemiology and clinical course of infectious mononucleosis will aid the GP in refraining from intervening when confronted with such a diagnosis).

General practitioners should, where possible, keep unlikely diagnoses under their own control

Here again, the general practitioner is faced with a dilemma. On the one hand there is a need to be open with the patient in sharing diagnoses and agreeing further management. On the other hand it is necessary to keep unlikely hypotheses as far as possible under control and only to pass on the burden of knowledge when it is strictly necessary. In achieving this balance the general practitioner can reduce the likelihood of unnecessary concern, or of a patient adopting a sick role when it is not appropriate.

THE DESIGN OF THE CHECKLISTS

The checklists presented in this part refer to some new complaints as well as to check-ups for chronic complaints. In both cases the content is limited to actions that take place in one consultation between the general practitioner and patient.They were drawn up on the basis of literature study and consensus discussion by experienced general practitioners. Some of them include information from the new national standards devised by the Dutch College of General Practitioners (Grol 1990*a*).

Use of the checklists

It may be that practitioners will wish to photocopy the checklists and use them when observing consultations, marking off the items covered. This is not to say that every item should be covered on each occasion, but the check can form a basis for discussion—and repeated omission of an item may be noteworthy. Alternatively readers may wish to adapt the checklists, omitting some items and adding others.

Another way of using the checklists would be to take out the records of several patients with a condition, for instance a chronic condition, and review the completeness of the items entered in the record as having been carried out. In the peer group the practitioners could review their data in relationship to others—or all the data could be pooled with each doctor only knowing their own figures.

Whether used in consultation analysis with a colleague or as a basis for discussion in a peer group the essential steps are for the practitioner to review present performance, decide optimal performance, and begin to make changes to improve.

More information on the methodology can be found in Chapters 8, 9, and 11.

HYPERTENSION FOLLOW-UP

Practitioners will need to decide their own frequency for checking each item (suggest: * every visit, # yearly, ● five-yearly) and action to be taken if a finding is not normal.
The following items may need to be considered:

Enter: ■ (done), □ (omitted), ▨ (not indicated)

History	1	2	3	4	5	6
* Well-being	□	□	□	□	□	□
* Physical complaints	□	□	□	□	□	□
* Any side-effects	□	□	□	□	□	□

Examination/investigation
* Blood pressure	□	□	□	□	□	□
* Weight/Quetelet index	□	□	□	□	□	□
# Chest examination	□	□	□	□	□	□
# Fundoscopy	□	□	□	□	□	□
# Urinary protein	□	□	□	□	□	□
# Blood creatinine	□	□	□	□	□	□
● Blood cholesterol	□	□	□	□	□	□

Also consider:
– chest X-ray	□	□	□	□	□	□
– ECG	□	□	□	□	□	□
– ambulatory blood pressure	□	□	□	□	□	□

Management/education
* Discuss medication concerns	□	□	□	□	□	□
* Discussion management/change	□	□	□	□	□	□
* Follow-up arrangements made	□	□	□	□	□	□
# Check self-care/lifestyle: – smoking	□	□	□	□	□	□
– weight/diet	□	□	□	□	□	□
– alcohol	□	□	□	□	□	□
– exercise	□	□	□	□	□	□

DIABETES FOLLOW-UP

Practitioners will need to decide their own frequency for checking each item (suggest: * every visit, # annually, ● every five years) and action to be taken if a finding is not normal.
The following items may need to be considered:

Enter: ■ (done), □ (omitted), ☑ (not indicated)

History	1	2	3	4	5	6
* Well-being	□	□	□	□	□	□
* Physical complaints	□	□	□	□	□	□
* Dietary problems	□	□	□	□	□	□
* Medication problems	□	□	□	□	□	□
# Exercise	□	□	□	□	□	□
# Smoking habit	□	□	□	□	□	□
# Pruritus	□	□	□	□	□	□
# Pain/paraesthesia in legs	□	□	□	□	□	□
# Sexual problems	□	□	□	□	□	□
# Visual problems	□	□	□	□	□	□
# Angina	□	□	□	□	□	□
# Claudication	□	□	□	□	□	□

Examination/investigation						
* Fasting blood glucose	□	□	□	□	□	□
* Urinary protein/glucose	□	□	□	□	□	□
* Quetelet index	□	□	□	□	□	□
* Blood pressure	□	□	□	□	□	□
* Visual acuity	□	□	□	□	□	□
# Fundoscopy	□	□	□	□	□	□
# Inspection of feet: – circulation	□	□	□	□	□	□
– reflexes	□	□	□	□	□	□
# Blood creatinine	□	□	□	□	□	□
● Blood cholesterol	□	□	□	□	□	□

Management/education						
* Discussion of immediate concerns	□	□	□	□	□	□
* Discussion of current management	□	□	□	□	□	□
* Follow-up arrangement made	□	□	□	□	□	□
# Check self-care/lifestyle: – self-monitoring	□	□	□	□	□	□
– foot/eye care	□	□	□	□	□	□
– smoking habit	□	□	□	□	□	□
– diet	□	□	□	□	□	□
– exercise	□	□	□	□	□	□
● Advise to join patients' society	□	□	☑	□	□	□

ASTHMA FOLLOW-UP

The frequency of follow-up depends on the severity of the asthma, medication use, number of exacerbations, etc. Well-stabilized patients with asthma probably do not need review more than yearly.
The following items may need to be considered:

Enter: ■ (done), □ (omitted), ⊿ (not indicated)

History	1	2	3	4	5	6
Well-being	□	□	□	□	□	□
Physical complaints:						
– recent exacerbations	□	□	□	□	□	□
Current level of treatment	□	□	□	□	□	□
Problems with medication	□	□	□	□	□	□
Smoking habit	□	□	□	□	□	□
Restrictions on lifestyle:						
– e.g. exercise tolerance	□	□	□	□	□	□
Time off work/school	□	□	□	□	□	□

Examination/investigation						
Chest examination	□	□	□	□	□	□
Current peak flow (PF):						
– as percentage of best and predicted	□	□	□	□	□	□
– before and after bronchodilators	□	□	□	□	□	□
Consider spirometry	□	□	□	□	□	□
Inhaler technique	□	□	□	□	□	□
Review of home recordings of PF	□	□	□	□	□	□

Management/education						
Discuss any concerns:						
– provide printed information if required	□	□	□	□	□	□
Consider other tests, e.g. allergy	□	□	□	□	□	□
Agree management programme:						
– self-management protocol	□	□	□	□	□	□
– action in emergency	□	□	□	□	□	□
Arrange follow-up	□	□	□	□	□	□

CHEST PAIN

Causes include cardiac, pulmonary, musculoskeletal, gastrointestinal, neuro-
logical, and functional.
The following items may need to be considered:

Enter: ■ (done), □ (omitted), ☑ (not indicated)

History	1	2	3	4	5	6
Recent precipitating event	□	□	□	□	□	□
History of pain	□	□	□	□	□	□
Characteristics of pain	□	□	□	□	□	□
Accompanying symptoms:						
– e.g. cough, breathlessness, gastrointestinal, palpitations, anxiety	□	□	□	□	□	□
Smoking habit	□	□	□	□	□	□
Precipitating factors, e.g. fears	□	□	□	□	□	□
Examination/investigation						
Pulse, blood pressure	□	□	□	□	□	□
Cardiovascular system	□	□	□	□	□	□
Chest	□	□	□	□	□	□
Chest wall	□	□	□	□	□	□
Abdomen	□	□	□	□	□	□
Management/education						
Share diagnosis	□	□	□	□	□	□
Share prognosis	□	□	□	□	□	□
Agree management:						
– behaviour	□	□	□	□	□	□
– drugs	□	□	□	□	□	□
– referral	□	□	□	□	□	□
Follow-up arrangement if necessary	□	□	□	□	□	□

COUGH

Causes include infection, inflammation (including smoking), asthma, cardiac failure, chronic chest disease, foreign body, malignancy.
The following items may need to be considered:

Enter: ■ (done), □ (omitted), ⊘ (not indicated)

History	1	2	3	4	5	6
Nature and cause of complaint	□	□	□	□	□	□
Duration of complaint	□	□	□	□	□	□
Predisposing factors (night-time, exercise)	□	□	□	□	□	□
Associated dyspnoea or wheeze	□	□	□	□	□	□
Additional symptoms (fever, weight loss)	□	□	□	□	□	□
Sputum	□	□	□	□	□	□
Smoking habit	□	□	□	□	□	□
Therapies already tried	□	□	□	□	□	□

Examination/investigation						
Examination of throat and ears in children	□	□	□	□	□	□
Examination of lungs	□	□	□	□	□	□
Examination of cardiovascular system	□	□	□	□	□	□
Peak flow, before and after B agonist	□	□	□	□	□	□
Chest X-ray	□	□	□	□	□	□
Sputum culture	□	□	□	□	□	□
Specific investigations	□	□	□	□	□	□

Management/education						
Share diagnosis	□	□	□	□	□	□
Share prognosis	□	□	□	□	□	□
Advise against smoking	□	□	□	□	□	□
Use of medication:						
– codeine/expectorants	□	□	□	□	□	□
– antibiotics	□	□	□	□	□	□
– brochodilators/steroids	□	□	□	□	□	□
Agree referral if indicated	□	□	□	□	□	□
Arrange follow-up if indicated	□	□	□	□	□	□

DIARRHOEA

Causes include infection, food intolerance, inflammatory, obstruction, functional.
The following items may need to be considered:

Enter: ■ (done), □ (omitted), ☑ (not indicated)

History	1	2	3	4	5	6
Nature of complaints	□	□	□	□	□	□
History and duration of complaints	□	□	□	□	□	□
Associated symptoms, e.g. weight loss, fever	□	□	□	□	□	□
Recent events or travel	□	□	□	□	□	□
Other affected family members	□	□	□	□	□	□
Occupation, e.g. food worker	□	□	□	□	□	□

Examination/investigation						
General impression	□	□	□	□	□	□
Signs of dehydration	□	□	□	□	□	□
Examine abdomen	□	□	□	□	□	□
Culture faeces	□	□	□	□	□	□
Faecal occult bloods	□	□	□	□	□	□
Blood tests	□	□	□	□	□	□
Barium studies/endoscopy	□	□	□	□	□	□
Specific tests, e.g. fetal fat, jejunal biopsy	□	□	□	□	□	□

Management/education						
Share diagnosis	□	□	□	□	□	□
Share prognosis	□	□	□	□	□	□
Advise diet/fluids	□	□	□	□	□	□
Use of medication:						
– electrolyte replacement	□	□	□	□	□	□
– anti-diarrhoeal agents	□	□	□	□	□	□
– antibiotics	□	□	□	□	□	□
Specific therapies	□	□	□	□	□	□
Referral if indicated	□	□	□	□	□	□
Follow-up arrangements if indicated	□	□	□	□	□	□

HEADACHE

Causes include tension headache, migraine, referred pain (e.g. sinus, teeth, cervical spine), intracranial pressure (hypertension, tumour, meningitis), temporal arteritis.

The following items may need to be considered:

Enter: ■ (done), □ (omitted), ◩ (not indicated)

History	1	2	3	4	5	6
History of complaint	□	□	□	□	□	□
Characteristics of pain	□	□	□	□	□	□
Exacerbating or associated factors	□	□	□	□	□	□
General health, well-being	□	□	□	□	□	□
Specific questions:						
– (e.g. prodrome and migraine, respiratory tract infection in sinus pain)	□	□	□	□	□	□
Therapies already tried	□	□	□	□	□	□
Psychosocial problems	□	□	□	□	□	□

Examination/investigation						
Blood pressure	□	□	□	□	□	□
Local possible sources of pain:						
– (e.g. sinuses, temporal arteries, teeth, cervical spine, ears)	□	□	□	□	□	□
Neurological examination	□	□	□	□	□	□
Blood tests, e.g. erythrocyte sedimentation rate	□	□	□	□	□	□
X-ray chest/cervical spine/CT scan	□	□	□	□	□	□

Management/education						
Share diagnosis	□	□	□	□	□	□
Share prognosis	□	□	□	□	□	□
Discussion of self-help, e.g. relaxation	□	□	□	□	□	□
Use of medication:						
– analgesics	□	□	□	□	□	□
– anti-migraine	□	□	□	□	□	□
– anti-depressant	□	□	□	□	□	□
– specific for primary cause	□	□	□	□	□	□
Agree referral if indicated:						
– counsellor/specialist	□	□	□	□	□	□
Follow-up arrangements if indicated	□	□	□	□	□	□

LEG ULCER

The following items may need to be considered:

Enter: ■ (done), □ (omitted), ▨ (not indicated)

History	1	2	3	4	5	6
Time since ulcer developed	□	□	□	□	□	□
Predisposing cause	□	□	□	□	□	□
Previous history:						
– of ulcer/varicose veins or arterial disease	□	□	□	□	□	□

Examination/investigation						
Examine ulcer (position, size, margin)	□	□	□	□	□	□
Examine for varicose veins	□	□	□	□	□	□
Examine for oedema	□	□	□	□	□	□
Doppler test to distinguish arterial/venous ulcer	□	□	□	□	□	□
Other cardiovascular examination	□	□	□	□	□	□

Management/education						
(For venous ulcers)						
Advise self-help:						
– leg elevation	□	□	□	□	□	□
– exercise	□	□	□	□	□	□
Treat underlying problems:						
– cardiac failure	□	□	□	□	□	□
Dressings and bandaging	□	□	□	□	□	□
Agree referral if indicated	□	□	□	□	□	□
Arrange follow-up if indicated	□	□	□	□	□	□

LOW BACK PAIN

The following items may need to be considered:

Enter: ■ (done), ☐ (omitted), ◩ (not indicated)

History	1	2	3	4	5	6
Duration of pain	☐	☐	☐	☐	☐	☐
Characteristics of pain:						
– radiation	☐	☐	☐	☐	☐	☐
– exacerbating activities	☐	☐	☐	☐	☐	☐
– past history of pain	☐	☐	☐	☐	☐	☐
Work situation/situation at home	☐	☐	☐	☐	☐	☐
Consequences in terms of daily functioning	☐	☐	☐	☐	☐	☐

Examination/investigation						
Inspect back:						
– scoliosis	☐	☐	☐	☐	☐	☐
– muscle spasm	☐	☐	☐	☐	☐	☐
Palpate back:						
– bones, joints	☐	☐	☐	☐	☐	☐
Straight leg raising test	☐	☐	☐	☐	☐	☐
Neurological examination of legs	☐	☐	☐	☐	☐	☐
Examine abdomen	☐	☐	☐	☐	☐	☐
Blood tests, e.g. erythrocyte sedimentation rate	☐	☐	☐	☐	☐	☐
X-ray of lumbar spine and pelvis	☐	☐	☐	☐	☐	☐
Specific investigation of abdominal/pelvic causes:						
– e.g. urine examination, renal/pelvic ultrasound	☐	☐	☐	☐	☐	☐

Management/education						
Discussion of immediate concerns	☐	☐	☐	☐	☐	☐
Discussion of current management	☐	☐	☐	☐	☐	☐
Follow-up arrangement made	☐	☐	☐	☐	☐	☐
Check self-care/lifestyle:						
– self-monitoring	☐	☐	☐	☐	☐	☐
– foot/eye care	☐	☐	☐	☐	☐	☐
– smoking habit	☐	☐	☐	☐	☐	☐
– diet	☐	☐	☐	☐	☐	☐
– exercise	☐	☐	☐	☐	☐	☐
Advise to join patients' society	☐	☐	☐	☐	☐	☐

ACUTE OTITIS MEDIA

Policies vary between countries and practices.
The following items may be considered in managing any episode:

Enter: ■ (done), □ (omitted), ⊠ (not indicated)

History	1	2	3	4	5	6
General condition	□	□	□	□	□	□
Pain	□	□	□	□	□	□
Discharge from ear	□	□	□	□	□	□
Fever	□	□	□	□	□	□
Recent upper respiratory tract infection	□	□	□	□	□	□
Frequency of episodes	□	□	□	□	□	□
Hearing between episodes	□	□	□	□	□	□
At risk?						
– e.g. age, Down's syndrome, immunocompromised	□	□	□	□	□	□

Examination/investigation						
Examine both tympanic membranes	□	□	□	□	□	□
Examine nose/throat for congestion	□	□	□	□	□	□
Assess level of distress	□	□	□	□	□	□
Bacteriology swab if discharge	□	□	□	□	□	□

Management/education						
Use of:						
– analgesics	□	□	□	□	□	□
– antibiotics	□	□	□	□	□	□
– referral	□	□	□	□	□	□
Discuss disease and its course	□	□	□	□	□	□
Discuss immediate concerns	□	□	□	□	□	□
Discuss current management	□	□	□	□	□	□
Follow-up arrangements made	□	□	□	□	□	□
Advise lifestyle/self-care:	□	□	□	□	□	□
– water/swimming	□	□	□	□	□	□
– further consultation	□	□	□	□	□	□

SORE THROAT

The following items may need to be considered in managing any episode:

Enter: ■ (done), □ (omitted), ◪ (not indicated)

History	1	2	3	4	5	6
Nature of complaint	□	□	□	□	□	□
Duration	□	□	□	□	□	□
Associated symptoms	□	□	□	□	□	□
Fever, malaise, rash	□	□	□	□	□	□
Prior medication	□	□	□	□	□	□
Smoking habit	□	□	□	□	□	□
Immunocompromised?	□	□	□	□	□	□
Relevant past history, e.g. rheumatic fever	□	□	□	□	□	□

Examination/investigation

Inspect neck/throat	□	□	□	□	□	□
Palpate cervical glands	□	□	□	□	□	□
Other examinations:						
– e.g. rash, spleen	□	□	□	□	□	□
Throat swab	□	□	□	□	□	□
Blood count	□	□	□	□	□	□
Infectious mononucleosis blood test	□	□	□	□	□	□

Management/education

Use of:	□	□	□	□	□	□
– analgesics	□	□	□	□	□	□
– antibiotics	□	□	□	□	□	□
– symptomatic remedies	□	□	□	□	□	□
Discuss disease and its cause	□	□	□	□	□	□
Discuss immediate concerns	□	□	□	□	□	□
Discuss management plan	□	□	□	□	□	□
Follow-up arrangements if necessary	□	□	□	□	□	□

URINARY TRACT INFECTION

Management depends on patient's age, sex, and frequency of attacks.
The following items may need to be considered:

Enter: ■ (done), □ (omitted), ⊠ (not indicated)

History	1	2	3	4	5	6
Nature of symptoms/signs including:						
– dysuria	□	□	□	□	□	□
– frequency	□	□	□	□	□	□
– haematuria	□	□	□	□	□	□
– pain	□	□	□	□	□	□
– fever	□	□	□	□	□	□
General well-being	□	□	□	□	□	□
Recurrent symptoms?	□	□	□	□	□	□
Vaginal/penile discharge?	□	□	□	□	□	□

Examination/investigation						
Palpate kidneys	□	□	□	□	□	□
Vaginal examination	□	□	□	□	□	□
Urine dipstick nitrite	□	□	□	□	□	□
Urine bacteriology	□	□	□	□	□	□
Vaginal/urethral swabs	□	□	□	□	□	□
Renal X-ray/ultrasound	□	□	□	□	□	□
Blood creatinine	□	□	□	□	□	□

Management/education						
Alternative diagnoses e.g. atrophic vaginitis, urethral syndrome, VD	□	□	□	□	□	□
Use of:						
– antibiotics	□	□	□	□	□	□
– analgesics	□	□	□	□	□	□
– treatment of associated cause	□	□	□	□	□	□
– referral	□	□	□	□	□	□
– prophylaxis	□	□	□	□	□	□
Discuss nature and prognosis of complaint	□	□	□	□	□	□
Discuss management plan	□	□	□	□	□	□
Check self-care/lifestyle:						
– adequate fluid intake	□	□	□	□	□	□
– voiding after intercourse	□	□	□	□	□	□
Follow-up arrangements if necessary	□	□	□	□	□	□

17 Instruments for evaluating management in general practice

INTRODUCTION

Following consultation skills and clinical performance the management of the practice is a third central aspect of general practice care. A wide area must be considered, including: practice equipment, organization of services, staff organization, communication and co-operation with colleagues, teamwork, medical recording and finance, and information technology.

Practice management is increasingly perceived as a crucial aspect in the provision of care in general practice. It largely determines the satisfaction of the patients with the general practitioner and the practice, continuity of care, and the efficiency and effectiveness of the provided services. It deserves full attention in quality assurance and improvement and should be an interesting aspect of general practice, but unfortunately GPs often consider it an annoying necessity. Yet it can be addressed well in peer review activities, in particular by using peer visiting methods with colleagues (see Chapter 11).

In order to help providers of primary care in carrying out a good review of practice management, a selection of instruments is presented in this chapter. These help to determine the lines along which various fields of practice management could be reviewed. Likewise, existing instruments could be added to form a tailored package for peer review.

INSTRUMENTS FOR REVIEW OF PRACTICE MANAGEMENT

Practice management differs considerably between and within countries because of the healthcare system, the local setting, the specific nature of the practice (health centre, group, solo practice), and the availability of staff. Despite these differences the organization of practice has much in common that can serve as a basis for review.

In developing instruments for reviewing practice management, draft guidelines were first developed based on literature analysis and interviews with experts (van den Hombergh 1993). After the main areas of concern had been identified and ordered (see box on p. 151), every aspect of general practice care considered to be relevant for practice management was subsequently allocated to one of the areas. In this way a complete systematic and practical list of aspects and items related to practice management was developed.

This 'checklist' was tested in a consensus procedure with 25 experts in the field and 15 regular GPs. They commented on the relevance and validity of the items as

Framework for review of practice management

Equipment
- building and premises;
- equipment;
- equipment in the car.

Delegation and teamwork
- staff (receptionists/nurses/assistants);
- GP colleagues;
- primary care network;
- consultants and hospitals;
- other providers of care.

Organisation of services
- reception and accessibility;
- surgeries and home visits;
- routines for referrals and prescriptions;
- organization of preventive care.

Medical and financial administration
- medical record keeping;
- fnancial administration.

Quality management
- guidelines and criteria development;
- data collection and evaluation of care;
- improving practice performance.

well as the usefulness of the list for the profession. Specific instruments were drawn up on the basis of this list and information derived from instruments developed in other countries (Royal College of General Practitioners 1985).

In a pilot 70 GPs visited each other in their practices and used these new instruments. The findings of this pilot were used to modify the instruments. Some of the instruments are presented in this book, in a somewhat adapted version to make a broad application possible (Table 17.1).

The items in the various instruments are put in such a way that the answer 'yes' mostly has a positive connotation. This makes a quick visual impression of the scores possible. However, the scores on the instruments cannot be used as 'hard' criteria for evaluating the quality of practices. They mainly serve educational purposes for learning about and improving practice management.

Table 17.1   *Instruments for review of practice management*

Aspect of care	Instrument
Use of equipment	Questionnaire for GP
Equipment in the car	Observation by peer
Tasks of practice nurse, assistant, receptionist	Questionnaire for staff
Organization of services	Questionnaire for GP
Provision of services	Questionnaire among a sample of patients
Health education	Observation by peer
Medical record keeping	Chart audit by a peer or a practice assistant
Quality management	Questionnaire for GP

The instruments will be found most useful if they have been completed first and are then considered in peer group discussions. Trainees will also find them helpful in obtaining a better idea of what practice management may entail.

Use of equipment: questionnaire for the GP

Do you use these items regularly (e.g. at least once a month)?

Tuning fork ☐
Nasal speculum ☐
Quetelet index (body-mass index, BMI) calculator/chart ☐
Audiometer ☐
An auriscope ☐
Disposable local anaesthetic for the eye ☐
Doppler meter ☐
Tonometer for ocular pressure ☐
Proctoscope ☐
ECG ☐

Do you carry out these procedures regularly (e.g.
at least once quarterly)?

Communicate with a patient using an interpreter ☐
Assess the lung function with a peak flow meter/spirometer ☐
Treat a patient with hypostatic ulcer with supportive bandages ☐
Insert a catheter into the bladder ☐
Freeze a wart/skin lesion with liquid nitrogen ☐
Tape or bandage a sprained ankle ☐
Measure blood sugar in the surgery/office ☐

Equipment in the car: observation by a peer

How many of these vials are present in the doctor's bag?

Atropine ☐ Morphine (or analogue) ☐
Adrenaline ☐ A corticosteroid ☐
Antihistamine ☐ Penicillin ☐
Diclofenac injection ☐ A phenothiazine ☐
Glucagon or glucose 50% ☐ Diazepam ☐

Total number present in the kit _____ vials
Total number of vials not yet out of date _____ vials

Are these items present in the kit?

An inventory of the vials ☐
Referral letters paper ☐
A diagnostic stick for urine examination (not expired) ☐
A diagnostic stick for blood glucose (not expired) ☐
A thermometer ☐
A sterile catheter and anaesthetic gel ☐
A simple mucus extractor (oral suction) ☐
A tampon to stop severe epistaxis ☐
A β agonist as a spray or nebulizer ☐
Rectal diazepam ☐

Tasks of practice nurse: questionnaire for nurse/assistant

Technical tasks: do you carry out these items regularly?

Removal of sutures ☐
Venepuncture ☐
Ear syringing ☐
Liquid nitrogen application for warts ☐
Follow-up of patients with high blood pressure ☐
Cardiovascular risk assessment ☐
Taking cervical smears ☐
Bandaging or strapping a sprained ankle ☐
Application of glue or steri strips to small wounds ☐
Audiometry ☐
Sight testing ☐
Taking an ECG ☐
Pressure bandaging a leg ulcer ☐

Laboratory: do you carry out any of these examinations regularly?   ☐

Measurement of blood glucose level   ☐
Measurement of erythrocyte sedimentation rate   ☐
Testing of faeces for occult blood   ☐
Blood leucocyte count   ☐

Information giving: is it your task to?

Give advice in common complaints such as diarrhoea,cough,   ☐
common cold, flu, fever, or urinary tract infection
Assess and counsel patients with specific diseases such as diabetes,   ☐
increased cardiovascular risk, or asthma
Please enter how often you hand out printed information to
patients per week   _____ times/wk

Administration: is it your task to?

Assess whether a patient requires a home visit   ☐
Enter notes in the patient's record after a consultation   ☐
Assist your GP on call   ☐
Check the contents of the GP's emergency bag   ☐
Manage chronic disease or preventive programmes   ☐
Make claims for items of service   ☐

Management:

How many hours a week do you spend on communication in the
practice discussing matters concerning practice management
and organization?   _____ hrs/wk

Do you write out prescriptions for common complaints?   ☐
Do you have written guidelines for your chronic disease management?   ☐
Do you make referrals for simple indications?   ☐
Do you share responsibility for the follow-up of patients in high-risk   ☐
groups?

Organization of services: questionnaire for the doctor or practice manager

What is the average consultation time?   _____ min.
How many office consultations did you do in the past month?   _____
How many home visits did you do in the past month?   _____
Do you have a practice manager?   ☐
Do you have a secretary?   ☐

Do you have a facilitator or health visitor on site? ☐
Do you have a counsellor? ☐
Do you know the ethnic and social class distribution of the practice? ☐
Do you have an age-sex register? ☐
Do you keep a register of all diabetics? ☐
Do you keep a register of all patients with increased cardiovascular risk? ☐
Do you keep a register of all patients requiring flu vaccine? ☐
Do you keep a register of at-risk elderly? ☐
Do you offer special services for diabetics? ☐
Do you offer special services for asthmatics? ☐
Do you offer special services for health promotion? ☐
Have you reviewed telephone answering and delay? ☐
Have you reviewed the time delay for patients seeking appointments? ☐
Are there meetings with partners for education/quality improvement? ☐
Are there meetings with partners for day-to-day care or planning? ☐
Are there meetings with all staff for planning care? ☐
Are there meetings with all staff for quality improvement? ☐

Provision of services: patient questionnaire

In order to gain some information on the acceptability of the organization of the practice, the routines in the practice, the accessibility of the practice, and the services provided, a short questionnaire for patients is used. Patients are particularly able to give valuable feedback on certain aspects of practice management.

At least 25, preferably more than 50 patients, visiting the practice, are asked to complete the questionnaire after the consultation. This will *not* assure a reliable picture of patient satisfaction in the practice. However, it will show certain interesting findings that can be used for peer review and quality improvement activities.

Patient questionnaire

Access   **yes no**

1. Can you contact the practice immediately in case of an emergency? ☐ ☐
2. If you call early in the day can you always get a home visit on the same day? ☐ ☐
3. Can you obtain an appointment on the same day if you request it urgently? ☐ ☐
4. If you want to speak to your GP can you usually reach her/him by telephone the same day? ☐ ☐
5. Do you find the receptionist to be a barrier between you and your GP? ☐ ☐

6. Are the practice's arrangements for out-of-hours care made clear to you?   □ □
7. In case of a minor emergency (for example: ankle sprain, cuts and bruises, foreign body in the eye) do you prefer to go to your own general practice rather than to casualty?   □ □
8. When you come for an appointment how late is the GP usually running?   _____ min.
9. In your opinion is the consultation time on average sufficient?   □ □
10. Do you have a say in how long your consultation should be (5, 10, 15 minutes or more)?   □ □
11. Do you favour a first-come/first-served surgery as well as normal appointments?   □ □
12. Is your GP often interrupted by telephone calls?   □ □
13. Do you often have to see a GP who is not your usual GP during working hours?   □ □

Health education
14. When you need information about health concerns can you usually get it at the practice?   □ □
15. Have you been given printed information about your health problems following a consultation?   □ □
16. Does your GP ever use models or drawings to help with explanations?   □ □

Privacy
17. Can you make requests at the reception desk without being overheard?   □ □
18. Do you ever overhear conversations in the doctor's consulting room?   □ □
19. Does the privacy of your medical record cause you any concern?   □ □

Facilities
20. Do you consider hygiene in the practice good enough?   □ □
21. Do you have the impression that the practice is trying to be up to date professionally?   □ □
22. Do you feel that the practice equipment is adequately up to date?   □ □
23. Is the waiting room area comfortable and well equipped?   □ □

General remarks
Please comment on anything, good or bad, that you would like to say about the organization of the practice. We particularly welcome freehand comments.

The questionnaire should be handed out by the GP or the receptionist with some instructions (why it is being done; that it is anonymous and takes only a few minutes to complete; that it is valuable for the practice to know the opinions of the patients; and that it should be put sealed in a collecting box). It will not take much effort if one of the staff members will tally the answers and present them in an understandable way.

Health education: checklist for observation by a peer

Are the following available in the practice?

A demonstration model of the lumbar spine	☐
Diagrams to demonstrate internal anatomy	☐
A hand-out on hormone replacement therapy	☐
A hand-out on acne	☐
An explanatory leaflet on cardiovascular risks	☐
A diet sheet for constipation	☐
A patients' library containing at least ten books	☐
Systematic and accessible storage of health information material	☐

Medical records: check list for use in peer review

Assessing the medical records is an important aspect of peer review. The following method takes about one hour. You are requested to assess the records of at least 10 patients, for example:

two or more patients with diabetes mellitus;
two or more patients with a malignancy;
two or more patients with a history of heart attack or angina;
two or more patients with another chronic disease (like arthritis or obstructive airways disease);
two or more randomly selected patients.

If the practice uses computerized records with a terminal on the desk then you should use the computer screen also in completing the checklists. Some items will then score 100 per cent (e.g. readability).

	1	2	3	4	5	6	7	8	9	10	Total
General aspects											
1. Is the record in date order?	☐	☐	☐	☐	☐	☐	☐	☐	☐	☐	☐
2. Is the written text on the whole (>80%) readable?	☐	☐	☐	☐	☐	☐	☐	☐	☐	☐	☐

3.   Does the record   ☐ ☐ ☐ ☐ ☐ ☐ ☐ ☐ ☐ ☐ ☐
      show whether the
      consultations are
      home visits, telephone
      calls, or normal
      consultations?

Consultations
Select the last two
consultations with
meaningful data:

4.   Is the reason for   ☐ ☐ ☐ ☐ ☐ ☐ ☐ ☐ ☐ ☐ ☐
      encounter (S)
      recorded?

5.   Are investigations/   ☐ ☐ ☐ ☐ ☐ ☐ ☐ ☐ ☐ ☐ ☐
      examinations
      (O) recorded?

6.   Is the diagnosis or   ☐ ☐ ☐ ☐ ☐ ☐ ☐ ☐ ☐ ☐ ☐
      analysis of the
      problem (A) recorded?

7.   Is the plan (P), for   ☐ ☐ ☐ ☐ ☐ ☐ ☐ ☐ ☐ ☐ ☐
      treatment and
      follow-up recorded?

Select the last consultation
which resulted in a
prescription and check:

8.   Is it possible to   ☐ ☐ ☐ ☐ ☐ ☐ ☐ ☐ ☐ ☐ ☐
      determine accurately
      from the record all
      other medication the
      patient is taking?

9.   Is the dose of the   ☐ ☐ ☐ ☐ ☐ ☐ ☐ ☐ ☐ ☐ ☐
      prescribed medication
      recorded?

10.   Is the prescribed   ☐ ☐ ☐ ☐ ☐ ☐ ☐ ☐ ☐ ☐ ☐
      duration of the
      medication use
      recorded?

Chronic disease/ preventive care

11.   Does the record   ☐ ☐ ☐ ☐ ☐ ☐ ☐ ☐ ☐ ☐ ☐
      system include a
      summary?

12. Is there a separate flow-card for any major illness? □ □ □ □ □ □ □ □ □ □ □

13. Is the family history clear? □ □ □ □ □ □ □ □ □ □ □

14. Is the patient's preventive care risk profile recorded? □ □ □ □ □ □ □ □ □ □ □

15. Is the patient's occupation recorded? □ □ □ □ □ □ □ □ □ □ □

Quality management: questionnaire for the GPs in the practice or peer review group

Which of the following quality improvement activities are undertaken regularly by yourself or in your practice?

Regular quality meetings/quality circles □
– how often are the meetings _____/month
A staff member or partner with particular responsibility for □
quality improvement
A strategic plan for the practice with specific aims and actions □
Quality projects/ audits in the practice □
– how many in the last year _____
Systematic, continuous data collection in the practice □
Practice protocols for major areas of preventive care or chronic □
disease management
Joint planning meetings with hospitals/ other care providers □
Patient surveys/ patient involvement □
A complaint system for patients □
An annual plan for continuing medical education for each care provider □
An annual report on the practice □
Mutual practice visits by peers □
Help of facilitators for improving the practice □
Arrangements with insurers or local health authorities on quality □
(contracts, budget)

References

Audet, A., Greenfield S., and Field M. (1990). Medical practice guidelines: current activities and future directions. *Annals of Internal Medicine*, **113**, 709–14.

Baker, R. (1988). *Practice assessment and quality of care*, Occasional Paper, No. 39. London: The Royal College of General Practitioners, London.

Baker, R. and Presley, P. (1990). *The practice audit plan.* The Severn Faculty of the Royal College of General Practitioners, Bristol.

Bandura, A. (1986). *Social foundations of thought and action.* Prentice Hall, Englewood Cliffs.

Bartlett, E. (1983). Behaviour diagnosis: a practical approach to patient education. *Patient Counseling and Health Education*, **4**, 29–35.

Batalden, P. and Buchanan, E. (1989). Industrial models of quality improvement. In *Providing quality care: the challenge to clinicians* (ed. N. Goldfield and D. Nash), pp. 133–55. American College of Physicians, Philadelphia.

Batstone, G. (1990). Educational aspects of medical audit. *British Medical Journal*, **301**, 326–8.

Becker, M. and Green, L. (1975). A family approach to compliance with medical treatment: a selective review of the literature. *International Journal of Health Education*, **18**, 173–83.

Becker, M. (1985). Patient adherence to prescribed therapies. *Medical care*, **23**, 539–55

Becker, M. and Rosenstock, I. (1984). Compliance with medical advice. In *Health care and human behaviour* (ed. A. Steptoe and A. Matthews). Academic Press, New York.

Berwick, D. and Coltin, K. (1986). Feedback reduces test use in a Health Maintenance Organisation. *Journal of the American Medical Association*, **255**, 1450–54.

Berwick, D. (1989). Continuous improvement as an ideal in health care. *New England Journal of Medicine*, **320**, 53–6.

Berwick, D. (1992). Heal thyself or heal thy system: can doctors help to improve medical care? *Quality in Health Care*, Suppl. S2–S8.

Berwick, D., Godfrey, B., and Roessner, J. (1990). *Curing health care.* Jossey-Bass, San Francisco.

Berwick, D., Enthoven, A., and Bunker, J. (1992). Quality management in the NHS: the doctor's role—I and II. In *Audit in action* (ed. R. Smith). British Medical Journal, London.

Birmingham Research Unit of Royal College of General Practitioners (1977). Self-evaluation in general practice. *Journal of the Royal College of General Practitioners*, **27**, 265–70.

Black, N. (1990). Quality assurance of medical care. *Journal of Public Health Medicine*, **12**, 97–104.

Branthwaite, A., Ross, A., Henshaw, A., and Davie, C. (1988). *Continuing education for general practitioners*, Occasional Paper, No. 38. The Royal College of General Practitioners, London.

Cameron, R. and Best, A. (1987). Promoting adherence to health behavior change interventions: recent findings from behavioral research. *Patient Education Counseling*, **10**, 139–54.

Cervero, R. (1981). A factor analytic study of physicians' reasons for participating in continuing education. *Journal of Medical Education*, **56**, 29–34.

Cohen, D., Jones, P., Lettenberg, B., and Neuhauser, D. (1982). Does cost information availability reduce physician test usage? *Medical Care*, **20**, 286–92.

Crombie, D. and Fleming, D. (1988). *Practice activity analysis*, Occasional paper, No. 41. Royal College of General Practitioners, London.

Deming, W. (1986). *Out of the crisis*. MIT-CAES, Cambridge, Mass.

Difford, F. (1990). Defining essential data for audit in general practice. *British Medical Journal*, **300**, 92–100.

Donabedian, A. (1980). Explorations in quality assessment and monitoring. Vol. I. Ann Arbor, Michigan: Health Administration Press.

Donabedian, A. (1986). Criteria and standards for quality assessment and monitoring. *Quality Review Bulletin*, **12**, 99–108.

Eisenberg, J. (1985). Physical utilization. The state of research about physician practice patterns. *Medical Care*, **23, 4**61–83.

Ellis, R. and Whittington, D. (1993). *Quality assurance in health care. A handbook*. Edward Arnold, London.

Essex, B. and Bate, J. (1991). Audit in general practice by a receptionist: a feasibility study. *British Medical Journal*, **302**, 573–6.

Everett, G., De Blois, S., Chang, P. and Holets, T. (1983). Effect of cost education, cost audits and faculty chart review on the use of laboratory services. *Archives Internal Medicine*, **143**, 942–4.

Farmer, A. (1991). Setting up consensus standards for the care of patients in general practice. *British Journal of General Practice*, **41**, 135–6.

Field, M. and Lohr, K., (eds) (1990). Clinical practice guidelines: directions for a new agency. Washington D.C., National Academic Press.

Fineberg, H. (1985). Effects of clinical evaluation on the diffusion of medical technology. In *Institute of Medicine. Assessing medical technologies*. National Academic Press, Washington.

Fink, A., Kosecoff, J., Chassin, M., and Brook, R. (1984). Consensus methods: characteristics and guidelines for use. *American Journal Public Health*, **74**, 979–83.

Fishbein, M. and Azjen, J. (1975). *Beliefs, attitudes, intentions and behavior*. Addison Wesley, Reading, Mass.

Fleming, D. and Lawrence, M. (1983). Impact of audit on preventive measures. *British Medical Journal*, **287**, 1852–4.

Flora, J. and Farquhar, J. (1988). Methods of message design: experiences from the Standard Five Project. *Scandinavian Journal Primary Care* (Suppl.), **1**, 41–80

Forrest, J., McKenna, M., Stanley, I., Boaden, N,. and Woodcock, G. (1989). Continuing education: a survey among general practitioners. *Family Practice*, **6**, 98–107.

Fowkes, F. (1982). Medical audit cycle: a review of methods and research in clinical practice. *Medical Education*, **16**, 31–45.

Fowkes, F., Davies, E., Evans, K., Green, G., Hartley, G., Hugh, A., Nolan, D., Power, A., Roberts, C., and Roylance, J. (1986). Multicentre trial of four strategies to reduce use of radiological tests. *Lancet*, 15 February, 367–70.

Frame, P., Kowalich, B., and Dewellyn, A. (1984). Improving physician compliance with a health maintenance protocol. *Journal Family Practice*, **19**, 341–4.

Gehlbach, S., Wilkinson, W., Hammond, W., Clapp, N., Finn, A., Taylor, W., and Rodell, M. (1984). Improving drug prescribing in a primary care practice. *Medical Care*, **22**, 193–201.

Grant, G., Gregory, D., and Van Zwannenberg, T. (1985). Development of a limited formulary for general practice. *Lancet*, **i**, 1030–2.

Grivell, A., Forgie, H., Fraser, C., and Berry, M. (1981). Effect of feedback to clinical staff of information on clinical biochemistry requesting patterns. *Clinical Chemical*, **27**, 1717–20.

Grol, R. (1987). *Kwaleterksbewaking in de huisarrtsgenees kunde*. Thesis, University of Nijmegen, The Netherlands.

Grol, R. (ed.) (1988). *To heal or to harm*. Royal College of General Practitioners, London.

Grol, R. (1990a). National standard setting for quality of care in general practice: attitudes of general practitioners and response to a set of standards. *British Journal of General Practice*, **40**, 361–4.

Grol, R. (1990b). Peer review in primary care. *Quality Assurance in Health Care*, **2**, 119–26.

Grol, R. (ed.) (1991). *Intercollegiale toetsing van consultvaardigheden in de huisartspraktijk*. Bunge, Utrecht.

Grol, R. (1992a). Implementing guidelines in general practice care. *Quality in Health Care*, **1**, 184–191.

Grol, R. (eds.) (1992b). *Voorlichting door de huisarts*. NGH-publications, Utrecht.

Grol, R. and Heerdink, H. (1992c). De Bekerctheid mek en acceptalie van standaarden onder huisarben. *Huisarts & Weteuschap*, **35(3)**, 101–4.

Grol, R. (1993). Development of guidelines in general practice. *British Journal of General Practice*, **43**, 146–51.

Grol, R., Mesker, P., Schellevis, F. (eds.) (1988a). *Peer review in general practice*. Department of General Practice, Nijmegen.

Grol, R., Mokkink, M., and Schellevis, F. (1988b). The effects of peer review in general practice. *Journal of the Royal College General Practitioners*, **38**, 10–3.

Hall, J., Roter, D., and Katz, N. (1988). Meta-analysis of correlates of provider behavior in medical encounters. *Medical Care*, **26**, 657–75.

Haynes, R., Davis, D., Mc Kibbon, A. and Tugwell, P. (1984). A critical appraisal of the efficacy of continuing medical education. *Journal of the American Medical Association*, **251**, 61–4.

Haynes, B., Wang, E., and Da Mota Gomes, M. (1987). A critical review of interventions to improve compliance with prescribed medications. *Patient Education Counseling*, **10**, 155–166.

Irvine, D. (1990). *Managing for quality in general practice*. Kings Funds, London.

Irvine, D. and Irvine, S. (eds.) (1991). *Making sense of audit*. Radcliffe Medical Press, Oxford.

Kaplan, S., Greenfield, S., and Ware, J. (1989). Impact of the doctor–patient relationship on the outcomes of chronic desease. In: *Communicating with medical students* (ed. M. Stewart). Sage, Newbury Park.

Kincey, J., Bradshaw, P., and Ley, P. (1975). Patient satisfaction and repeated acceptance of advice in general practice. *Journal of the Royal College General Practitioners*, **25**, 558–66.

Klein, L., Charace, P., and Johannes, R. (1981). Effects of physician tutorials on prescribing patterns of graduate physicians. *Journal of Medical Education*, **56**, 504–11.

Kosecoff, J., Kanouse, D., Rogers, W., McCloskey, L., Wislow, C., and Brook, R. (1987). Effects of the National Institute of Health Consensus Development Program on physician practice. *Journal of the American Medical Association*, **258**, 2708–13.

Kottke, T., Rattista, B., De Friese, G., and Brekke, M. (1988). Attributes of successful smoking cessation interventions in medical practice. A meta-analysis of 39 controlled trials. *Journal of the American Medical Association*, **259**, 2883–9.

Lawrence, M. (1992). Audit and TQM in diabetic care in general practice. *Quality in Health Care*, **1** (Suppl.), 20–1.

Lawrence, M. and Schofield, T. (eds.) (1993). *Medical audit in primary health care*. Oxford University Press, Oxford.

Leape, L. (1990). Practice guidelines and standards. *Quality Review Bulletin*, **16**, 42–99.

Ley, P., Whiteworth, M., Skillbeck, C., Woodward, R., Pinsent, R., Pike, L., Clarkson, M., and Clark, P. (1976). Improving doctor–patient communication in general practice. *Journal of the Royal College General Practitioners*, **26**, 720–4.

Ley, P. (1982). Giving information to patients. In *Social psychology and behavioral medicine* (ed. J. Eiser) Wiley, Chichester.

Lomas, J. and Haynes, R. (1988). A taxonomy and critical review of tested strategies for the application of clinical practice recommendations: from 'official' to 'individual' clinical policy. In *Implementing preventive services* (ed. R. Battista and R. Lawrence). *American Journal of Preventive Medicine*, **4**, 77–95.

Lomas, J. (1990). Quality assurance and effectiveness in health care: an overview of quality assurance in health carre. *Quality Assurance in Health Care*, **2**, 5–12.

McIntyre, N. and Popper, K. (1983). The critical attitude in medicine: the need for a new ethics. *British Medical Journal*, **287**, 1919–23.

Marinker, M. (ed.) (1990). *Medical audit and general practice*. British Medical Journal, London.

Martin, A., Wolf, M., Thibodeau, L., Dzau, V., and Braunwald, E. (1980). A trial of two strategies to modify the test-ordering behavior of medical residents. *New England Journal of Medicine*, **303**, 1330–6.

Marwick, J., Grol, R., and Borgiel, A. (1992). *Quality assurance for family doctors*. WONCA, Jolimont, Australia.

Meichenbaum, D. and Turk, D. (1987). *Facilitating treatment adherence*. Plenum, New York.

Mills, G., Pace, R., and Peterson, B. (1988). *Analysis in human resource training and organization development*. Addison-Wesley, Reading, Mass.

Morisky, D., Green, L. and Levine, D. (1986). Concurrent and predictive validity of a self-reported measure of medication adherence. *Medical Care*, **24**, 67–74.

Morrell, D. (1991). Role of research in the development of organization and structure of general practice. *British Medical Journal*, **302**, 1313–6.

Morris, L. and Halperin, J. (1979). Effects of written drug information on patient knowledge and compliance: a literature review. *American Journal of Public Health*, **69**, 47–52.

Nelson, A. (1976). Orphan data and the unclosed loop: dilemma in PSRO and medical audit. *New England Journal of Medicine*, **295**, 617–20.

North of England Study of Standards and Performance in General Practice (1992). Medical audit in general practice. I. Effects on doctors' clinical behaviour for common childhood conditions. *British Medical Journal*, **304**, 1480–4.

Norton, P. and Dempsey, L. (1985). Self-audit: its effects on quality of care. *Journal of Family Practitioners*, **21**, 289–91.

Ovretveit, J. (1992). *Health service quality*. Blackwell Scientific Publications, Oxford.

Owen, P. and Allery, L., Harding, K., Hays, R. (1989). General practitioners' continuing medical education within and outside their practice. *British Medical Journal*, **299**, 238–40.

Palmer, R., Louis, T., Hsu, L., Peterson, H., Rothrock, J., Strain, R., Thompson, M., and Wright, E. (1985). A randomized controlled trial of quality assurance in sixteen ambulatory care practices. *Medical Care*, **23**, 751–70.

Parrino, T. (1989). The non-value of retrospective peer comparison feedback in containing hospital antibiotic costs. *Amerian Journal of Medicine*, **86**, 442–8.

Pendleton, D. (1983). Doctor–patient communication: a review. In *Doctor–patient communication* (ed. D. Pendleton and J. Hasler). Academic Press, London.

Pendleton, D., Schofield, T., Tate, P., and Havelock, P. (1984). *The consultation. An approach to learning and teaching*. Oxford University Press.

Pendleton, D., Schofield, T., and Marimker, M. (1986). *In pursuit of quality*. London: The Royal College of General Practitioners.

Pickup, A., Mee, L., and Hedley, A. (1983). Obstacles to continuing education. *Journal of the Royal College General Practice*, **33**, 799–801.

Post, D. (1984). Farmacotherapeutische overleggroepen. *Medical Contact,* **39**, 1125–7.

Pringle, M., Bilkhu, J., Dornan, M., and Head, S. (1991). *Managing change in primary care.* Radcliffe Medical Press, Oxford.

Putnam, W. and Curry, L. (1980). Patient care appraisal in the ambulatory setting: effectiveness as a continuing education tool. *Annual Conference on Research in Medical Education,* **19**, 207–22.

Ramirez, A. and Shepperd, J. (1988). The use of focus groups in health research. *Scandinavian Journal of Primary Health Care* (Suppl.), **1**, 81–90.

Rogers, E. (1983). *Diffusion of innovations.* Free Press, New York.

Roter, D., Hall, J., and Katz, N. (1988). Patient–physician communication: a descriptive summary of the literature. *Patient Education and Counselling,* **123**, 99–119.

Rosser, W. (1983). Using the perception–reality gap to alter prescribing patterns. *Journal of Medical Education,* **58**, 728–32.

Royal College of General Practitioners (1985). *What sort of doctor? Assessing quality of care in general practice,* Occasional Paper, No. 23. The Royal College General Practitioners, London.

Royal College of General Practitioners (1990). *Fellowship by assessment.* Occasional Paper, No. 50. The Royal College General Practitioners, London.

Royal New Zealand College of General Practitioners (1990). Quality Assurance Programme Reference. General Practice Training Programme. Royal New Zealand College of General Practitioners, Wellington.

Sackett, D. and Snow, J. (1979). *The magnitude of compliance and non-compliance with therapeutic regimens.* Hopkins, Baltimore.

Sackett, D., Haynes, R., and Tugwell, P. (1985). *Clinical epidemiology,* Little, Brown, Boston/Toronto.

Schillemans, L., De Grande, L., and Remmen, R. (1989). Using quality circles to evaluate the efficacy of primary health care. In I*nternational innovations in evaluation methodology* (ed. R. Conner and M. Hendricks). Jossey-Bass, San Francisco.

Sanazaro, P. Determining physicans performance. Continuing medical education and other interacting variables. *Evaluation and the Health Professions,* **2**, 197–210.

Schroeder, S., Myers, L., McPhee, S., Showstack, J., Simborg, D., Chapman, S., and Leong, J. (1984). The failure of physician education as a cost containment strategy. *Journal of the American of Medical Association,* **252**, 225–30.

Shaw, C. (1980). Aspects of audit: the background. *British Medical Journal,* **280**, 1256–8.

Sheldon, M. (1982). *Medical audit in general practice,* Occasional Paper, No. 20. Royal College of General Practitioners, London.

Shirriffs, G. (1989). Continuing educational requirements for general practitioners in Grampian. *Journal of the Royal College of General Practitioners,* **39**, 190–2.

Smith, R. (ed.) (1992). *Audit in Action.* British Medical Journal, London.

Smits, A., Meyboom, W., Mokkink, H., Van Son, J., and Van Eyk, J. (1991). Medical versus behaviour skills: an observation study of 75 general practitioners. *Family Practice,* **8**, 14–8.

Sommers, L., Sholtz, R., Sheperd, R., and Stark Weather, D. (1984). Physician involvement in quality assurance. *Medical Care,* **12**, 1115–34.

Soumerai, S., McLaughlin, T. and Avorn, J. (1990). Quality assurance for drug prescribing. *Quality Assurance in Health Care,* **2**, 37–58.

Sprij, B., Casparie, A., and Grol, R. (1989). Interventiemogelijkheden om een verandering in de medische praktijkvoering te bewerkstelligen. Wat is effectief? *Ned Tijdschr Geneesk,* **133**, 1115–7.

Stein, L. (1981). The effectiveness of continuing medical education; eight research reports. *Journal of Medical Education*, **56**, 103–10.

Stolline, A. and Weiner, J. (1988). *The new medical marketplace*. Johns Hopkins University Press, Baltimore.

Van den Hombergh, P. (1993). *Check-lijst en toetsinstrument praktijkvoering*. University of Nijmegen.

Van de Rijdt-van de Ven, T., Touw, A., Vermuë, M. (1988). *Peer group performance review for general practitioners*. Stichting O & O, Utrecht.

Verby, J., Holden, P., and Davies, R. (1979). Peer review of consultations in primary care: the use of audiovisual recordings. *British Medical Journal*, **1**, 1686–8.

Wandless, I., Mucklow, J., Smith, A. (1979). Compliance with prescribed medicines: a study of elderly patients in the community. *Journal of the Royal College of General Practitioners*, **29**, 391–6.

WHO (World Health Organization) (1993). *Continuous quality development: a proposed national policy*. WHO, Copenhagen.

Williamson, J. (1994). Health care quality management in the 21st century. In *Evaluation of quality assurance in medicine* (ed. H-K. Seibmann). Bleicher Verlag, Gerlinger Germany (forthcoming).

Winkens, R., Pop, P., Grol, R., Kestex, A., and Knottnerus, J. (1992). Effect of feedback on test ordering behaviour of general practitioners. *British Medical Journal*, **304**, 1093–6.

Winkler, J., Lohr, K., and Brook, R. (1985). Persuasive communication and medical technology assessment. *Archives of Internal Medicine*, **145**, 314–7.

Winnickhoff, R., Collin, R, and Morgan, (1984). Improving physician performance through peer comparison. *Medical Care*, **6**, 527–34.

Wones, R. (1987). Failure of low-cost audits with feedback to reduce laboratory test utilization. *Medical Care*, **25**, 78–82.

Index